Why Can't PEOPLE Just Do Their Jobs?

ROBERT A. HEATH, SR.

Why Can't People Just Do Their Jobs?

The Empowering Leader's Guide to Having More Fulfillment, Less Stress, and Getting the Best out of Those You Lead

Robert A. Heath, Sr., Esquire

Difference Press

McLean, Virginia, USA

Copyright © Robert A. Heath, Sr., 2018

Difference Press is a trademark of Becoming Journey, LLC

In association with Legacy Academy Press, LLC

Allendale, Michigan, USA

All rights reserved. No part of this book may be reproduced in any form without permission in writing from the author. Reviewers may quote brief passages in reviews.

Published 2018

DISCLAIMER

No part of this publication may be reproduced or transmitted in any form or by any means, mechanical or electronic, including photocopying or recording, or by any information storage and retrieval system, or transmitted by email without permission in writing from the author.

Neither the author nor the publisher assumes any responsibility for errors, omissions, or contrary interpretations of the subject matter herein. Any perceived slight of any individual or organization is purely unintentional.

Brand and product names are trademarks or registered trademarks of their respective owners.

Cover Design: Jennifer Stimson

Editing: Todd Hunter

Author photo courtesy of TK

To God, the Source of all inspiration, I pray that I am a worthy messenger. To the giants upon whose shoulders I stand, thank you for your legacy. And to any who would read, understand, and implement these words, blessings, joy, and peace along your journey. Welcome to the Legacy Leadership Path!
#LegacyLeadership.

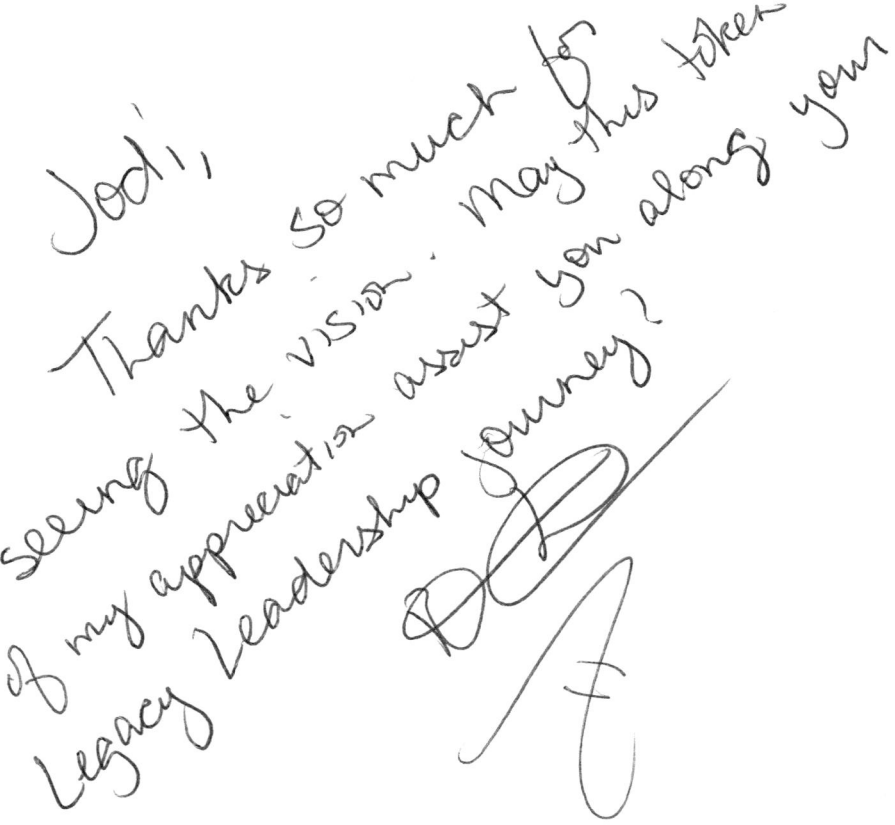

Jodi,
Thanks so much for seeing the vision. May this token of my appreciation assist you along your Legacy Leadership Journey!

9-14-21

Table of Contents

Introduction	- 7 -
Chapter 1: Turning Point	**- 20 -**
My Leadership Journey	- 20 -
Chapter 2: The Leader's Way	**- 31 -**
The EMPOWER Method	- 31 -
Chapter 3: The Empowering Leader	**- 41 -**
The Foundation of the Legacy Leadership	- 41 -
SECTION 1: VISION	**- 57 -**
Chapter 4: Begin with the End In Mind	**- 58 -**
(E)MPOWER: Examine and Evaluate Your Expectations	- 58 -
Chapter 5: Matrix Moments	**- 77 -**
E(M)POWER: Measure Expectations	- 77 -
SECTION 2: COMMUNICATION AND STRATEGY	**- 96 -**
Chapter 6: Many Hands Make Light Work	**- 97 -**
EM(P)OWER: Proper Delegation a.k.a. Play to Win	- 97 -
Chapter 7: Resilience Is the Foundation of Success	**- 117 -**
EMP(O)WER: Optimize Your Environment for Growth	- 117 -
SECTION 3: TACTICS, TECHNIQUES, AND PROCEDURES	**- 139 -**
Chapter 8: The "S" in BAMCIS	**- 140 -**
EMPO(W)ER: Watch and Learn	- 140 -
Chapter 9: You Don't Want to Have All the Answers	**- 158 -**
EMPOW(E)R: Engage Their Inner Problem Solver	- 158 -
Chapter 10: You Get More of What You Focus On	**- 166 -**
EMPOWE(R): Reward What You Want to Continue	- 166 -
Chapter 11: Simple Does Not Equal Easy	**- 181 -**
Obstacles, Pitfalls, and Worst-Case Scenarios	- 181 -
SECTION 4: LEGACY	**- 198 -**

Conclusion	- 199 -
Cultivating Resiliency...	- 199 -
Acronym Glossary	- 209 -
Further Reading	- 211 -
Acknowledgments	- 212 -
About the Author	- 215 -
Thank You	- 217 -

Introduction

It was 6:30 in the evening on a Thursday, and Andrew was still at work.

He was supposed to leave work by 5:00 p.m. He and his wife Jasmine had plans. It was date night. Time for dinner and a movie. Three weeks prior, they had made arrangements to hire a babysitter. Every time they talked about the date, Jasmine would light up. They would finally be free to just enjoy the night. It seemed it had been so long since they were able to just enjoy themselves. They had both been looking forward to this for a while.

This was going to be their first date in three months. Keeping this one was really important considering he had to reschedule their last two. This time was going to be different, he thought. He had made Jasmine a promise, and he was really trying to keep it. He had worked hard, and he was excited this morning because thought he was going to be able to be home on time.

That was until around three in the afternoon when he read the email from one of his team members, Jeremy.

Jeremy was a graphic designer for the firm. As the Executive Accounts Director for their mid-sized marketing firm, Andrew had a team of about ten people that he led. Jeremy was one of those that worked directly for him. Andrew had a proposal to give to an existing client regarding a new service his firm was offering. Jeremy was handling the slides for Andrew's presentation because this one needed to be good. He was also supposed to put together a couple of detailed graphics slides to highlight the pros of choosing Andrew's proposal over the other proposals the client is considering. Normally, Jeremy does good work on the flyers, posters, and social media campaigns they put out. Andrew thought this shouldn't be much different. It should have been easy for him. This presentation was not for a huge account, but it was an important one. Jeremy, however, had never worked on a presentation of this scale with Andrew, even though it was part of his job description.

***

Andrew gave Jeremy over three weeks to prepare this proposal, which was quite extensive. When they met, Andrew explained to Jeremy the entire project. He made sure that Jeremy had all the information that he needed to get the work done.

At the end of the briefing, Andrew asked Jeremy if he had any questions.

"Nope, I've got it. If I have any questions, I'll reach out," Jeremy said at the end of their meeting.

***

Andrew didn't want to micromanage Jeremy, so he tried to leave him alone for much of those three weeks. He was aware that Jeremy was very busy during the week that he gave him the proposal, so he didn't even ask him to start it that week, "just to review it and let me know if you have questions."

Andrew met with Jeremy again the next week to go over some extra requirements he had for the project. He also checked in with Jeremy later that week to remind him of the deadline and ask if he had any questions.

"Nope, I've got it."

Andrew just had this feeling, though. He had an intuition that he should get Jeremy to show him the graphics slides because those had to be right for the presentation to go well. So, yesterday morning, Andrew sent Jeremy an email asking to see the graphics on the proposal. No response. Jeremy was out of the office in meetings all yesterday afternoon, so they weren't able to review the graphics together.

***

Jeremy's deadline for having the proposal to Andrew was 11:00 this morning. At 10:00 a.m., Jeremy sent Andrew an email asking to have until the end of the day to get the proposal in. "I have most of it done. I just need to finish up the graphics," he said.

"I should make him stop right now and come to my office," Andrew thought. Then he remembered that he has another meeting in five minutes. "It can wait," he thought. "I don't want to make Jeremy feel like I don't trust him."

"Besides, why should I have to fix everything all the time? This is Jeremy's job. He can do it."

So he gave him the extra time, but in his email, he let him know that he wanted to have the proposal no later than 3:00 p.m.

Jeremy sent the proposal via email at 3:05.

As he reviewed the slides and the graphics, Andrew realized the work Jeremy gave him was acceptable, but it did not do three things that he specifically asked for–the three things that Andrew needed it to do. He called Jeremy into his office to discuss.

As he and Jeremy discussed why the presentation wasn't correct, Jeremy said, "Those things weren't in the original proposal information. How was I supposed to know that they needed to be done like that?"

Andrew reminded Jeremy that they discussed these things the second week that they went over this. It was something that they had discussed at length on that day, and Jeremy had said he had no questions. Jeremy replied, "Oh, I must've forgot about that. I didn't start working on the project until this week since I had those other projects you gave me, and I just went off of what you emailed me."

Andrew explained to Jeremy that he needed him to get this work done so that he could have time to practice his presentation. Jeremy let Andrew know that he could stay until 5:00 p.m., but he had to get his kids from daycare at 5:30, and he was leaving right after to visit family out of town for the next five days.

Andrew knew that he could make Jeremy stay until the work was finished, but then they would have had to pay him overtime and staying late would have also created a problem with his family. Jeremy was a widowed, single father with two kids. He was taking his kids to see his parents who live out of state. They couldn't travel much, and he had this trip planned for three months.

So, Andrew and Jeremy worked on making sure the graphics were good before Jeremy left, but then Andrew still had to do the other work to make it right. He had to make sure that the presentation was in the right order and that it worked the way that it was supposed to. Andrew was going to be in meetings all day tomorrow, and then, he had to travel on the weekend for the presentation. He only had access to all of his tools and his data while he was at the office.

And so at 6:30 p.m., Andrew was still at work. Andrew didn't know how he was going to make sure this didn't happen in the future, but he knew that he and Jeremy were going to have a long talk when they got back to the office the next week.

***

He called his wife to let her know that he would be late. "Probably around 7:30," he explained. She was understandably disappointed.

"Don't cancel the babysitter. I promise, I'll be home soon. We can grab something quick for dinner and maybe still make the later show."

She was not happy, but she said OK. She explained that she knew that his job was important, but sometimes she just wished he would make the family a priority–make her a priority.

Andrew felt terrible. He had promised her that it wouldn't be like this. Two years into this position and he was still working late more often than coming home on time or early. This wasn't how it was supposed to be. Andrew had always wanted to be a leader. He always liked helping people. He was always a team player, and he truly believed in his team. He knew that they were capable of more than they were currently doing. But it had been two years, and it didn't seem to be improving. His was putting in more time and feeling more stress than before he became a leader.

At dinner time, his wife was constantly having to answer the question "Where's Daddy?" and she didn't like it. He missed every school event that took place during the work day, and he could rarely get away even for parent-teacher conferences.

He knew that this couldn't go on. The kids were going to be starting sports and plays and other extracurricular activities. He had promised himself that he would be around more for his kids than his parents were.

***

As he finished up the presentation, he thought of all the times that he had to stay late to fix problems that his team members should have solved. He thought about all the times that he had to rush in and save the project so that it would meet the standards of excellence that were expected of him and his team. He thought about the fact that he could never really leave work at work. It pained him that his wife constantly felt like he was not there, even when he was at home, because his mind was always on work.

He thought about the classes that he had been to, the week-long seminars he had attended, the online leadership courses he had taken. He had always learned useful information from these, but he always seemed to come back to this same place. He couldn't seem to get over the hump. He could never get the results that he wanted from his team and the results he knew they were capable of without nearly doubling his output. He just wasn't as effective a leader as he wanted to be, as he knew he could be, and he was beginning to lose his passion for leadership. He was beginning to wonder if he even wanted to be a leader at all.

Andrew knew other executives that seemed to be able to get their people to do great work and could still go home and spend time with their families. He even knew a couple of people from his networking group, with teams that were bigger than his, that got together to play golf every Friday afternoon.

He couldn't remember the last time he was able to play golf during the week. He couldn't even remember the last time he was able to leave the office early. He wondered what it must feel like to be able to leave and trust that everything would be okay. Heck, even on his weekends, he was always figuring out ways to put out fires from work. He was beginning to wonder if work-life balance was a real thing.

***

As he left the office, he was full of frustration, doubt, and anger. The following thoughts kept racing through his head:

"Why can't my people just do their jobs?"

"Dan doesn't have this problem with his graphics guy!"

"If Jeremy would have just done what I told him, this wouldn't have been a problem!"

"Why don't my people want to work as hard as I do?"

"It's so frustrating that I feel like I want them to be successful more than they do."

"It always seems like I have to do everything, or it doesn't get done right."

"Maybe you can't teach people to be successful?"

"Maybe there are just lazy people and then there are those of us who can be successful?"

"Maybe you are just born with it?"

"Am I wasting my time trying to get them to be more productive, trying to get them to grow?"

***

Does this sound similar to any of the encounters you have had with your team? Have you had the same thoughts and feelings and questions that Andrew had?

You try to treat people like you want to be treated. You treat your people with respect. You make reasonable requests. You ensure that your instructions are clear. You provide them with all the tools they need to get the job done.

You try to give them a good model. You come early. You stay late. You give them a demonstration every day of what you expect from them. You lead by example.

However, it just doesn't seem to work in the long run. You may get good production from them for a time, but it never seems to last. You just can't count on them to do what they are supposed to when it counts.

Your employees seem like they get what you are asking for in meetings. They say all the right things. And, when you are in the office, they do all the right things. However, whenever you have a day or two where your schedule takes you out of the office for an extended time, or heaven forbid, you go on vacation, when you come back, the office is worse than when you left it.

Is your current situation beginning to make you feel trapped? You can't leave, you can't rest, and you can't take any time off. You can't work on the things that you want to work on because you constantly have to check up on the work they are supposed to be doing.

Maybe it's the accounts manager that you hired six months ago to straighten out your accounts receivable. He came with great recommendations, and sure, he can handle the basic accounts. However, if it is an account that requires a little bit of original thought and problem solving to deal with, it feels like he doesn't know that it is his job to fix it. That is unless you are there to answer his questions, things just don't get done.

Or, maybe you have had a sales manager working under you for the past year and a half. She understands the job. She is good at closing the deal, but she just can't seem to begin to anticipate the simple things that would allow her to reach her full potential and meet the growth numbers you want to meet this year. She just seems to do the bare minimum of what is necessary. You can't leave her for too long without ensuring that she is doing exactly what she is supposed to do. If you try to treat her like a manager and don't check up on her routinely, then she starts dropping the ball on major accounts.

You have some members on your team who are just not carrying their weight. They are not living up to the expectations that you had for them, the things they told you they could do. They are not excelling, and they are barely fulfilling the job description. They are just getting by. They know it, and you know it.

For whatever reasons, you can't replace them. Maybe you are dealing with a hiring freeze. Maybe they have a contract. Maybe they are in a union. Maybe you know that they need the job and that they have some issues going on at home that are affecting work performance. Whatever it is, you just don't feel like you can let them go.

And what's even worse, if you were to let them go, you are not sure how you would train their replacement. What if you go through all the work of firing them and hiring someone else only to have the exact same problems just six months to a year later?

You are caught between a rock and a hard place. You have a job (or jobs) that are not being done correctly, and it is beginning to affect the entire team. Not only are you having to do more work to cover up for their lack of initiative and follow-through, other members on your team are having to step up as well. And they are not happy. They know who the "coasters" are, and they are getting tired of having to pull double duty for the sake of the team.

It is costing you productivity. It is costing you money. It is costing you increased stress and anxiety. It is costing you time–

specifically, time with your family and friends. And, it is costing you the respect of your team. The longer this goes on, the worse it gets.

Perhaps this has even cost you a couple of good team members already. And who can blame them, right? If you weren't so invested here, you might have left already too. But you are committed. You aren't going anywhere.

And part of the reason that you aren't going anywhere is because, deep down, you know that it won't really matter. People are the same no matter where you go, and if you go to another company, you know that you will have to deal with the same issues. You saw this at the other places that you worked, before you were in charge.

It wasn't you, but you saw people do the same things. On your end, you made sure that you were not part of the problem. You turned in your work on time. You went above and beyond. You put the mission of the team above your personal goals.

You worked hard, and you felt the increased stress of having to carry the weight of those who didn't. This work ethic and attitude is what got you to where you are today. You can still remember vowing that when you became a leader you wouldn't let that happen on your team.

Yet, here you are. You know that this is a problem that you have to fix. There has to be a solution. You know in your gut that you can turn this around. You have to. You know that if this keeps going, it's not a question of "if" you burnout but "when."

You just wish that you could get through to your team. If you could just get them to see themselves the way you see them, it would change everything. If you could get them to take their work seriously and think outside the box. If you could get them to anticipate problems and be part of the solution.

Can you imagine for a second if your people took more initiative and ownership over their performance? If they just did their jobs the way they know they should, the way they were trained, the way you have explained to them over and over again? If they completed projects without you having to spell everything out and check up on them constantly, what would that be like? It would be great, right?

Would it change the way things run around the office?

Of course! It would free you up to do so much more for your company and for your team. The team would be so much more productive, and you would finally have the time to work on those projects that you have been putting on the back burner for the past year. You could mentor them more and get them prepared for larger roles. You could negotiate for raises and promotions for them. You could be the type of leader that you have always wanted to be.

And how would it change your life?

You could finally get some tasks–especially those that you should not still be doing–off of your desk. You could go home at the end of the day and not have a full inbox and a to-do list that goes on forever. You could actually unplug.

You could finally take a vacation with your family without having to check in on work every day that you are gone. You might even be able to leave the office early and pick your kids up from school because you know your team is capable of taking care of everything without you there. Your stress levels would go down. You would have more time to start taking care of your body and your health properly. You wouldn't have to feel like you have to choose between your work and your home life. You could have balance.

If your team took more ownership of their roles and their growth, you would actually enjoy coming to work again. Mondays wouldn't be such a drag. You would look forward to working with your team and helping them to grow, instead of constantly being disappointed when you have higher hopes for them than they have for themselves.

How great would that be?

Are you ready to find out how you can make it happen for you and your team? Well, in the next chapter, I am going to let you know just how I overcame this very same issue and how you can too.

Chapter 1: Turning Point

"In a chronically leaking boat, energy devoted to changing vessels is more productive than energy devoted to patching leaks."--Warren Buffett

My Leadership Journey

How do I know that story so well? Well, it's because it was mine for a very long time. I was asking those same questions.

I had been studying leadership and how to help people manifest their greatness for the better part of the last twenty years, and these questions were still perplexing to me. Even with all that studying, it seemed that the better I got, the more successful I was, the harder I had to work.

And even though I like to work hard and I love helping people to achieve great results, I was beginning to realize that I just would not be able to sustain the pace I was on. I couldn't keep getting the results I was getting and continue to work as much as I was. Additionally, everything I was studying about leadership confirmed for me that continuing on this path was a recipe for disaster.

The point where it all clicked for me really happened about three years ago. I call it my culmination event. My leadership transformation really came together with my appointment to command of Company B, Headquarters and Support Battalion, for Marine Corps Base Camp Lejeune, and the struggles I overcame during that tour.

***

Over the three years before assuming command of Company B, I had worked as the Dean's Fellow at my law school after graduating with honors, spent nearly a year in my various Marine Corps Schools enduring the grueling physical and mental training necessary to become a Marine Corps officer, and then served for nearly two years as a defense counsel in the busiest defense office in the Marine Corps. Over that time, I had become the winningest defense counsel in the Camp Lejeune Defense Services Organization, winning 70% of the cases that I took to trial.

Safe to say that I was pretty good at what I did. I was good at accomplishing, at executing. I was an expert at being a do-er. I set goals, and I accomplished them.

By the time I assumed command, I had developed a resume and a reputation for being capable. This reputation was one of the main reasons that I was given command at a time that would see the battalion commander and the commanding general of our organization turn over. Basically, I was taking command of a company in transition in an organization that was about to get the equivalent of all new district and regional management.

Immediately upon taking command, I realized that I was in a different world than the one I had known before. I went from being in charge of myself to commanding a team of five and a company of over 200. Sure, I had been responsible for the development of one or two junior Marines and a couple of junior officers in our defense shop, but mostly, it was just me.

Now, as company commander, I was now responsible for the training and development of 220 Marines and sailors, along with my own staff. In addition to this shift, I was a relatively young captain, who had been a Marine for about a total of six years and only on active duty for about three. My inexperience was also compounded by the fact that the majority of the people I was leading had been in the Marine Corps longer than me. Many of them even outranked me. Though I still technically retained positional authority, it was an overwhelming situation.

Even in my company office, in a staff of five including myself, three of the other four Marines had been in the Marine Corps nearly twice as long as I had, and on active duty for three or four times as long. It would be an understatement to say that I had moments where I doubted whether I was qualified to lead them. However, I spoke to my mentors and those who selected me for the position, and they reassured me that I was the right person for the job.

***

The people that I led appeared to me to be very capable individuals. I had a team of two staff noncommissioned officers (you have to get approved by Headquarters Marine Corps to reach this rank), two senior noncommissioned officers with nearly nine years in the Marine Corps, and one lance corporal. However, it quickly became apparent to me that, while they were more than capable of doing their jobs, the way that they did things was nowhere near up to their capability. They were performing well below their potential.

This was also the case throughout the broader organization, which was made more troublesome due to the fact that it consisted of twenty-five different sections spread out across three bases. Considering these facts, it should have come as no surprise to me that the standard of work that we did as a company was lackluster. But I was surprised. I knew they were capable of more, and that was my expectation from day one.

To be clear, so as not to give you the impression that we were a lost cause, we were proficient. No one was in jeopardy of losing their jobs or being court martialed for dereliction, but our performance as a whole was well below optimal. We were performing very poorly compared to other companies in the battalion. This was affecting both our reputation and our ability as a staff to serve our troops.

As one example of our suboptimal performance, our readiness levels (the number of people in our company who were deemed fit and ready to be deployed for combat) hovered around 70%. The battalion goal for readiness was a minimum of 85%. Obviously, we were well below that. While this was a problem throughout the battalion, we were in last place at 74%, and that was something that had to change. So, like any other problem I had faced in my career, I looked at our objectives, set goals, and went about working to achieve them.

It was not a great start. In the space of four weeks, our readiness had actually dropped down to 70%. I wasn't getting people to report the way that they were supposed to, and they were not instituting the processes and systems that I had developed in order to get us to our objective. From the Marines in the company to my staff in the company office, it seemed that everyone was trying to do it, but no one was really getting it done.

***

One of the questions that continually resonated in my mind during this time was, "Why can't people just do their jobs?" And the next thought would be, "Why don't they respect me enough to do their jobs?"

I felt like I was doing all I could to help them. I was working hard. I was explaining the task as detailed as I could. I respected them enough to not micromanage them. I respected them enough to give them the time that they said they needed to get the job done. And still, they would not give me what they had promised. I knew they were capable. So in my mind, it must be a that they just didn't respect me.

***

Looking back now with the benefit of 20/20 hindsight, I can see that I homed in on the idea of respect because of some unresolved issues I had at the time. My thinking then was clouded by my feelings of inadequacy and unworthiness of the praise and accolades that I received.

It was then, and is still now, my sincere belief that respect is earned, not given. Therefore, I reasoned, if they were not giving me the respect that I thought I deserved, then I hadn't earned it. While I was right, it was not for the reasons that I thought. More about that later.

How did I get to this point? How did I become so accomplished but not feel like I was worthy of their respect? Well, you see, I am a recovering perfectionist. Specifically, I have battled Imposter Syndrome. Imposter Syndrome is when one has feelings of inadequacy that persist despite evident success. This is an issue that is very prevalent in high achieving, highly successful people who are unable to internalize their accomplishments, regardless of how successful they are in their fields.

That was me. This feeling of not being respected I am describing here had been a recurring theme throughout much of my adult life. Generally, I have felt well-liked, but often didn't feel respected. The lack of respect was my perfectionism's way of taking away my feeling of accomplishment. That's because Imposter Syndrome doesn't equate with low self-esteem or a lack of self-confidence. Imposters are plagued with chronic self-doubt and a sense of being undeserving of accolades and successes because of the link to perfectionism. This chronic self-doubt and sense of intellectual fraudulence supplanted any feelings of success or external proof competence.

This was my life. In my early years, I had been what many people would call successful. However, I never really appreciated my successes. Additionally, I began to see my ability to accomplish the tasks put before me as the main reason that I was valuable. Therefore, mistakes became intolerable, and failure was unthinkable. In my mind, my value was tied up into others' approval of me.

And then I went to college.

I went to college at 16, tested out of Calculus, and got an A on my first collegiate paper at the University of Illinois, one of the top public universities in the country. I definitely had the talent and ability to graduate from school with honors, if I had applied myself. But because so many people had told me college was hard and it wasn't, I felt let down. I no longer knew where the boundaries were. I mean, I had just pulled an all-nighter to get that A. No studying, no staying focused, just will and talent (in my mind). Also, being away from home and away from all the watchful eyes allowed me to not perform without any real consequences for the first time.

I would show them, I thought. Who cares about grades or going to class? I'm smart. I'm talented. I got this! I call this my rebellious phase.

I got my first taste of freedom from public scrutiny thanks to the fact that I was a full two hours away from home and from my parents.. My hubris got the best of me. I did the minimum I could to get by. And so, instead of being in the top of my class, I graduated with a 2.4 GPA which was only that high because in my junior year, after I withdrew mid-semester to keep from failing, it dawned on me that if I didn't start applying myself, I might not graduate.

Here is where my Imposter Syndrome battle really revved into high gear. I began to believe the narrative that the real me was lazy and not as good as everyone told me I was. Because of my experience, when I did graduate, I was ashamed to apply for graduate school and other programs. I could clearly see how my lack of discipline had cost me opportunities, and I was determined not to let that happen again. Of course, change without balance is just the other side of dysfunction. And so began my attempts to become worthy of being thought of as gifted.

I went from anti-authority, anti-establishment to the paragon of law and order. I went from being a free spirit to being part of the establishment. I became a teacher, an attorney, a Marine Corps officer, and a company commander. To be successful in these roles, in my mind, making mistakes was just not something that I could allow. To me, making mistakes meant that you were not qualified and not capable of doing your job. It also meant that you didn't respect the people you worked for or care about what you were doing. I couldn't be that lazy guy anymore. I had to work harder and do more than everyone else to prove that I was worthy.

Interestingly, success did not allow this feeling of unworthiness to subside for me. Over the following 10-year period, I got my Master's degree with a 3.82 GPA and my law degree, *cum laude*. I earned a commission as a Marine Corps officer, made Dean's list, was a T.A., won a Real Estate Development scholarship, and became Dean's fellow for the College of Law upon graduation. When I moved into practicing law, I continued to excel. I earned the record as the winningest Defense Counsel in the Camp Lejeune Defense Services Office.

These accomplishments didn't make the feeling of being an imposter go away. As a matter of fact, the more successful I became, the more I felt like I could not make mistakes. Because I had begun to see myself as the person who wasn't worthy if he made mistakes, I could not get relief. And it wasn't so much important to me whether others thought I made mistakes. If I thought I messed up or could have done better, that was unforgivable. And since I had a catalogue of all of my mistakes (we are our own best/worst critics), regardless of whether anyone else knew about them, I felt like I wasn't worthy of any of the praise or accolades that I received.

I knew when I should have studied harder. I knew when I turned in a paper late but didn't get penalized. I knew when I just got lucky in the courtroom and the opposing counsel didn't recognize my mistake. Much of my reputation, I felt, was based off of luck or things that I wasn't responsible for, characteristics that were passed down or learned. (I mean, that was all stuff I got from my pretty awesome parents, right?)

This was especially the case during my transition to becoming a company commander. And those early failures in the first four weeks of my command tour brought back all the feelings I had right after I graduated from college.

Maybe I should have been at work longer or done more. Though I had not been perfect, I felt like I was following all the rules yet not getting the results I wanted. And in my mind, it was because they didn't respect me. I just knew in my gut that they didn't respect me because I had not been perfect. I had not earned it.

Intellectually, I understood that this wasn't true. I knew it wasn't my job to be perfect. I knew that I could not do everything. I also understood that it was not efficient or effective to use my authority to make people do their jobs. I couldn't be everywhere at once, especially with this company. With over twenty-five different sections spread out over three different bases, it just wasn't realistic. I knew that even if I tried to do it all on my own, I could not make them get to our objective without sacrificing my entire life to my job, and that was unacceptable. But how could I get them to do their jobs if they didn't respect me and if they didn't care enough to do it on their own?

***

I was at my wit's end and at an emotional low point. I was worried about how my boss would think about my performance. I was worried that I was not leading my troops in a way that would make them successful. I was worried that everyone would finally see that I was an imposter and not really qualified to lead anyone.

As worried as I was, I was also angry at the fact that my people didn't seem to respect me enough to do what I was asking them to do. Why couldn't they see that what I had set up would make everyone's lives easier? Why couldn't they see that I had done most of the work? All they needed to do was follow the program.

Because I had tied people's respect for me (and my feelings of worthiness and purpose) to my accomplishments, performing poorly in this role was really creating a tremendous amount of inner turmoil for me. I didn't know it at the time, but this was the exact mix of circumstances and emotions that was necessary for me to be fed up enough to change. I didn't realize it then, but it was at that moment that I dedicated myself to making sure that this would not happen again.

And, it was at this point that everything seemed to click, and my life as a leader would never be the same.

Chapter 2: The Leader's Way

"What you're supposed to do when you don't like a thing is change it. If you can't change it, change the way you think about it. Don't complain." – Dr. Maya Angelou

The EMPOWER Method

In that moment, when I was beginning to doubt myself and my abilities, when I was really losing my passion and my confidence, I really got to thinking about who I wanted to be. I thought about what type of leader I wanted to be. I thought hard about the lessons that I had been learning throughout my life about how to lead people. I also truly took inventory of the things that I had accomplished and what I had to do to get to where I was.

It helped that at the time I was reading a number of different works on leadership. Many of them I was re-reading (something I highly recommend). A central theme began to shine through these books that I had not fully understood before. It kind of all hit me at once. And that idea, that theme was this: "It's not about YOU!"

Now I had heard this before and even taught it regarding personal accomplishment, but never did I get it with this level of understanding. Before, I always thought about this phrase in terms of being humble and sacrificing for the good of the group. But this was different. This new understanding was about leadership, about relationships, about interacting with those that you lead. It seemed that everything I had been struggling with up to this point was now crystal clear. It was one of those moments that feels like remembering something you knew long ago, while also encountering it for the first time.

I felt like a weight had been lifted off of my shoulders. In that moment, when I fully grasped this central concept of Legacy Leadership, that it's not about YOU! I realized that in all the books I had read and all the seminars I had attended, the point was not about sacrifice. It was about understanding one's true role as a leader.

From Lao Tzu's discussions of leadership in the *Tao de Ching* to Sun Tzu's words in *The Art of War,* to Dale Carnegie's stories in *How to Win Friends and Influence People* to Robert Kiyosaki's admonitions in *Rich Dad, Poor Dad,* to Steven Covey's *The 7 Habits of Highly Effective People,* to every John C. Maxwell book, it all hit me and seemed to make sense in that moment.

Leadership at its heart is not at all about the leader. Leadership is completely about the ability and the drive and the perseverance of the people. Therefore, it is the leader's job to do whatever he or she can to create an environment where their people can perform at their best and then get out of the way. It is about empowering and then letting go. That is the hallmark of true leadership: How well are the people able to work and accomplish their tasks without you? This was liberating for me to understand,

and it fundamentally changed the way that I approached my work as a company commander.

My first order of business was to look at the systems that I had put into place. I evaluated them based on how well they worked with the work schedules and battle rhythms of the groups that I led. I immediately saw how the dates that I requested information to be delivered were some of the worst dates for my staff during the week. Though they worked for me in the schedule that I had set up, they coincided with some of the group's busiest times. I was making them decide between doing what I was asking, which might have been a less urgent problem, and doing something that needed attention immediately.

This caused me to look at my staff deeper and assess how they went about their work. I saw how hard they worked and how much they cared. I saw that even if they were doing something in an inefficient way, it wasn't because they were resistant to change or because they were taking the easy route. They simply realized that they were not as good at doing what I had told them was better and more efficient way. When they tried, it made them feel slower and that made them feel like they were doing worse and letting the team down. That is why they didn't follow my systems.

Similarly, I looked at how I was having my staff report to me on their progress. Initially, I would go to them individually and check on their projects or have them come to me. This meant that, on the days that I didn't forget or get too busy to check in with them, I was taking ten to fifteen minutes out of their day and nearly an hour of my time to speak to each member of my team. This was tremendously inefficient. Not to mention, if their progress was not to the level that I had anticipated, that ten to fifteen minute meeting might go on for a half an hour. No wonder I was working seventy to eighty hours per week.

Additionally, they had no structure for when I was going to show up. Because of the numerous meetings I had at other locations throughout the week, my schedule had a number of variables in it. I would ask them to have things due by a certain day but not give a specific time. Then I would show up in the morning expecting it done, when they were planning to have it done by the end of the day. These were the things I began to see as I looked at my leadership from the perspective of my people. I began to see that there was a lot of miscommunication, a lot of uncertainty, a lot of expecting them to be mind-readers. Basically, there was much room for improvement.

It dawned on me that this might be why so few people were following through on what I needed them to do. I realized that there were a number of times in my planning where I overlooked important steps that were necessary for them to understand the vision the way that I did. I saw where I needed to bridge the gaps and how I needed to do a better job at actually setting them up for success.

***

Over the course of the next few months, I changed the way I led. I started by listening to what they felt were the obstacles in their path. Then I set about the task of doing my part to clear the obstacles which were in my purview.

I instituted a number of measures into our weekly routine: consistent staff meetings, clear measurable goals and timelines, contingency planning on the front end so that my staff knew what to do if things changed and I wasn't there. All of these things helped us to communicate better as a staff, and they helped the entire company to function better and more efficiently.

In the space of the next two months we increased our readiness numbers from 70% to 90%. Considering an upper limit of 93% (which was the highest readiness we could achieve on a perfect day due to administrative constraints on readiness like personnel who were transitioning out of the Corps, permanently on limited duty, and/or on maternity leave) this was more like 97% readiness. We had basically improved nearly 30% in two months. We went from last place to the highest readiness marks in the battalion.

A few months later, when the battalion commander was considering restructuring, Company B was selected to become responsible for nearly 200 more troops. This included moving the Commanding General's Headquarters group into our company. We had just gone from being the smallest company in the battalion to the largest, and our profile grew because everything we did had a direct effect on my boss's boss.

Because of the changes we made and the systems we put into place, the transition went over flawlessly. We were able to absorb the new troops, coordinate a barracks transfer, and maintain our readiness numbers without missing a beat.

By the end of my tour as commander of Company B, we were the best performing company in the battalion. My troops had gone from worst to first, and they had done so through some tough challenges. Our company staff had turned over by 60%. We also received an additional assignment of twenty troops attached to us from the Beach Patrol Detachment. Oh, and our barracks parking lot almost blew up (by no fault of anyone in our Company). But still my team charged on.

I too had made some significant changes and had grown a lot. I had gone from working twelve to thirteen hour days and most weekends, while taking home stress from the job, to having the time and the freedom to expand the services and programs we offered to our troops with no extra time added to my day. I was even able to eat dinner with my family nearly every night, something that hadn't happened regularly since before law school. To top it all off, at my change of command ceremony, I was honored by being awarded the Navy and Marine Corps Commendation Medal by my commanding officer.

I had figured out how to become the leader that I had always wanted to be. I had developed the greatness that was within my team. I had overcome my Imposter Syndrome, and I had learned how to help my team to shine, to lead in a way that set them up for success.

***

As I looked back over the journey that I took to get to that mountaintop, I saw that I was not alone in having these feelings, these struggles. I realized that many of my peers were going through the same thing. I also realized that a number of the books that I read dealt with leadership in a mostly abstract fashion. They discussed tactics and strategies for leadership, but the how of implementing those strategies seemed lightly addressed. What I believe to be the core concept of how to communicate and relate to those you lead was something I had to put together by taking bits and pieces from all of them.

I realized that there was a gap in the training that most of us receive along our leadership journeys. This gap becomes more evident when looking at the language that we use to describe what leaders do and how leaders think. This is the gap that I knew that I could fill. And that realization is what prompted me to create the Leader's Way and my EMPOWER Method.

This book is designed to help you make the transition from being focused on execution, a Do-er, to being a Leader. And not just any Leader, an Empowering Leader. Someone capable of helping those they lead to manifest the greatness that lies within them.

I will walk you through the relational and communication skills you need to master to ensure that you can get your team to take more initiative and have more follow-through. The techniques and management strategies that will allow you to have less stress and be more effective and efficient will also be covered. Ultimately, the EMPOWER Method will allow you to get the best out of the teams that you lead, regardless of who you lead.

Here's a synopsis of the EMPOWER Method:

E - Examine and Evaluate your Expectations

This step is about how to be clear on your vision as well as what your team is capable of right now. Sometimes you can fail before you start, especially if you begin with unreasonable expectations.

M - Measure their Expectations

Leaders have a tremendous responsibility to shape the vision and the perceptions of their team. Two very often overlooked components of this process are building trust and showing belief in your team. This chapter will show you how to do this and how to cultivate reciprocal treatment from your team members.

P - Play to Win with the Hand You are Dealt

The reality is that leaders don't often get to choose the members on their team. Even if they do, they don't get to choose the circumstances surrounding those teams. Here you will learn how you can assign roles and delegate tasks in such a way as to always maximize the strengths and minimize the weaknesses of your team, regardless of external factors and influences.

O - Optimize Your Environment for Growth

I will show you how to institute the appropriate feedback loops into your process. By using tools like Quality Control checks (QC checks) at optimal times, you are able to maximize your ability to influence your team while minimizing the amount of time and energy you need to expend to affect change. You will also exponentially increase the amount of opportunities you have to meaningfully interact with your team. This is a powerful skill set to master.

W - Watch and Learn

The goal in in this step is to completely shatter your understanding of supervision and your perception of how much involvement you should have during the execution phase of your plan. You will learn how little you are needed at this point and, more importantly, how many of the things that you currently do are really sabotaging your team's ability to perform without you.

E - Engage Their Inner Problem-Solver

The role of supervision and how to get your team to do more to find solutions to their problems is discussed here. This is the chapter where you move from teaching your people how to be more productive to teaching them how to think like leaders. You will help them cultivate the Leader's Mind and save them years off of their leadership journey.

R - Reward Your Team and Celebrate your Wins

This is the most crucial step for you to master if you want to have sustained growth and to truly create an environment where your people are routinely performing at their peak. Understanding the power of positive reinforcement is key to being an Empowering Leader. This lesson applies to all of the others.

I want to now give you some guidelines for the journey you are about to embark on. To become an EMPOWERing Leader, you must care like a Leader, you must think like a Leader, and you must act like a Leader. To do this you must develop these three components of the Empowering Leader:

- The Leader's Heart
- The Leader's Mind
- The Leader's Toolkit

Each of these three will be discussed in depth going forward. Make sure that you also think about how each step of EMPOWER relates to each component of Empowering Leadership. Some of the connections will be obvious, and some of them will require some reflection. That is OK. Remember: The learning is in the journey not the destination.

Chapter 3: The Empowering Leader

"Leadership is a journey from Execution to Empowerment." – Carla Harris

The Foundation of the Legacy Leadership

When I was in law school, I took my family to visit the Lincoln Museum in Springfield, Illinois. While I was there, I happened upon an essay wherein Lincoln was discussing the progress of man and our responsibilities to one another. In the essay, he made an analogy comparing our growth as humans to the path one takes to become the master of a trade. The beginning is the same for all, as an apprentice to a master. This is where our talents, abilities, and the tools of our trade are learned. The next step is to become a journeyman – in today's language, an independent contractor. Here, our talents are used to build a business reputation and to take care of ourselves and our families.

The final step is to become a master. The master is distinguished not by his ability to do but rather his ability to lead and teach. The master is distinct from the independent contractor in that the master creates work and opportunity for others, not just themselves. In doing this, the master is equally dependent on those whom he leads and teaches to accomplish his own goals. Moving from apprentice to independent contractor to master is the same journey that Steven Covey wrote about in *The 7 Habits of Highly Effective People*. It is the journey from dependence to independence to interdependence. Society is only marginally improved by the efforts of the journeyman, the individual. Society is exponentially improved by the work of the master, who works interdependently to impact the lives of people in the present and for generations to come.

The path of the Legacy Leader is the same. You start out as a Do-er aka Executing Leader. Then move onto Teacher aka Empowering Leader. The final transition is when you become a Master aka Legacy Leader! I call this The Leader's Way. This book will focus on that first transition, for this is where much of the pain of leadership is found. This is the reason so many of my clients come to me wondering, "Why can't my people just do their jobs?"

The reason for this is that our traditional education and professional development systems do not teach us how to lead. Though they prepare us to rise to positions of leadership, they do not introduce us to the Leader's Way. They prepare us for the Do-er's Way. Again, like Steven Covey discussed, our system likes to focus on the journey from dependence to independence, and by making that the goal, the process gets corrupted. The same is true with leadership.

We work through our schooling and our early careers to become very good at doing a particular thing. Whatever our trade is, there is one goal: to become as good at that trade as possible. Every system is designed to show you how to be a good Do-er. That is how you get recognized. That is how you get promoted.

Very few of our processes focus on how to become a great leader, even though there is a highly recognized need for the skill. Yet and still, you develop a reputation for yourself, then you are generally asked to lead others, and then treated like you should know how to do it.

While this promotion is supposed to signify the transition from Do-er to Teacher, this is rarely the case. Instead, this is the point in your journey where the most mistakes happen, and you get off track. This is where your superiors forget to inform you that you are being asked to move from Do-er to Teacher. Instead, you get promoted from Do-er to Manager or Supervisor. You get asked to perform in an Empowering Leader's role but you are given an Executing Leaders paradigm and tools. This misalignment is what this book is designed to overcome.

This book will show you how to make the necessary adjustments to move you back on the path of the Legacy Leader, the Leader's Way. You will get the training here that you should have gotten before you were asked to make the transition. As you progress through the program, you will see that the Leader's Heart, the Leader's Mind, and the Leader's Toolkit must be developed in order to make the transformation from Do-er to Teacher and not get stuck in Executing Leader (Do-er) mode. These components, and the paradigm shift necessary to obtain them, are the subject of our next section.

The Leader's Mind, a Paradigm Shift:

It is imperative that one appreciates the differences between the feelings, the thoughts, and the actions of an Empowering Leader in comparison with those of an Executing Leader. Many of the problems that you face with getting your team to take initiative and ownership of the projects that you give them can be traced to an incongruence among these three. As you read through this section, I want you to know that I understand your frustration and that it is reasonable to feel this way. You are experiencing what I like to refer to as the Manager's Dilemma. As this dilemma gets unpacked throughout this book, you will begin to see the source of much of your frustration.

The Manager's Dilemma: Mission vs Welfare

"2nd Platoon is up." It was 0400 (that's four in the morning in military time) and I and the other members of my Platoon were all accounted for and in the chow line. It was the third day of Range Week. This name is actually a bit misleading since Range Week is actually two weeks. Each day consists of mustering, eating chow, and lining up by 0510 each morning, with full gear and weapons, for a two-mile march to the range, ten to twelve hours of firing and classes at the range, and then a two-mile hike/run back to the barracks each evening.

The order had been given from the company commander that each Marine would eat breakfast in the chow hall every morning to ensure that we had adequate sustenance for the grueling training.

Because of the need for accountability, every platoon in the company had to have full accountability of its members by 0400 and had to ensure that each member did in fact eat breakfast. The only problem is that we went through the line in platoon order (1, 2, 3, 4, 5, 6), and each day the first platoon to eat from the previous day would cycle to the rear.

Logistically, it takes about ten minutes for each platoon to get through the line from payment to table. This means that the final platoon in the line generally gets about five to ten minutes to eat, depending on if any other personnel are in the line between the platoons. It also means that the last platoon is basically waiting to eat for the entire hour between 0400 and 0450 when they finally get to the head of the line. This did not sit well with many of my fellow platoon members, and so the problem was brought to the attention of our student platoon commander.

"Did the order say that we had to wait in line the entire time?" one of my fellow Lieutenants asked.

"No, but the CO (commanding officer) said that everyone had to go through the line," the student platoon commander responded.

"Well then, now that we have all checked in, can we go and eat in our rooms and then come back by 0440?" another Marine asked. Each Marine had a refrigerator and microwave in their room, which we stocked with food every weekend because the chow halls are not open 24/7. So, this was not an unreasonable request.

"No, we need everyone to stay here and wait in the line."

"But this is pointless, and we are tired, and we are just waiting. We can't eat until the other platoons have eaten, even if they are late," the Marine responded.

"That's just the way it has to be," the student platoon commander said with heaviness in his voice. You could see the struggle that he was going through. It was so simple but so difficult at the same time.

I asked, "Is that what is best for the platoon?"

His final answer is what we are going to discuss in this section: "It's not about what's best for the platoon. We have our orders, and so everyone has to stay here."

He was dealing with this dilemma and asking a question that many leaders will eventually face: If I have to choose between taking care of my people and accomplishing the mission, what's the right choice?

In the Marine Corps, as an officer, you are taught that the two most important things in leadership are mission accomplishment and troop welfare, in that order. A similar lesson is taught to rising leaders and management personnel in most successful organizations. On our route to becoming great at executing, at doing, we learn that the greater good is most important.

This is the lesson that actually begins to cultivate in us a sense that it is bigger than us. We begin to embrace a culture of looking after the greater good and being willing to sacrifice one's own needs for those of the team. We have many sayings in our culture that make this same point. There is no 'I' in team. It's not about you. Look at the bigger picture. This is how the Leader's Heart is formed.

However, in this process, by focusing on the mission, the diligent student is often left with a feeling that they can either focus on one or the other, either mission or welfare. This binary thinking is the hallmark of what I call the Manager's Mindset. For the Executing Leader, there is either the right way or the wrong way. They begin to see binary choices everywhere. This is where the leadership philosophy of "my way or the highway" comes from.

Executing Leaders, leading from the Manager's Mindset, like "best practices" and SOP's and clearly defined boundaries. For the Executing Leader, they resolve the dilemma of mission versus welfare easily. Mission first, last, and always. This was the perspective of the student platoon commander in the story above. He had his mission, and the most certain way of accomplishing it was to make sure that no one went anywhere once we had accountability.

Manager's Mind vs. Legacy Leader's Mind

The Manager's mindset is focused on the objective on execution. It is focused on accomplishment. It lives in the paradigm that we must sacrifice our own desires for the sake of the goal and that the goal is more important than anything. We know that the Manager's Mind is disciplined. We know that the Manager's Mind is focused. We know that the Manager's Mind is capable of getting the job done. We also know that the Manager's Mindset has not been working for you.

So how does the Leader's Mind differ and how does it help you to solve the Manager's Dilemma? The Leader's Mind expands on the truths that the Manager's Mind understands; however, it uses those truths for a greater purpose than simply accomplishing objectives. It is not that the Leader's Mind doesn't know or appreciate the lessons that the Manager's Mind knows; it is just that it has a different focus. And that focus makes all the difference.

The following chart illustrates the differences in focus between the Manager's Mind and the Leader's Mind.

Executive Leader's Focus	Empowering and Master Leader's Focus
Authority	Respect
The Leader	The Follower
The Mission	The Team
The Battle	The War
The Destination	The Journey
What is...	What could be...

Authority vs Respect

An Executive Leader, aka a Manager, is focused on the authority of their role and the responsibility that comes with that authority. From the Manager's Mind, it is difficult to understand why your team doesn't respect your authority and the authority of the system. It is difficult to comprehend why they can't just do their jobs, why they would have the audacity to leave a responsibility unfulfilled. To the Manager's Mind, authority is the source of respect, and those who don't respect authority are not worthy of respect.

When I was a kid, my father taught me a lesson that I believe sums up the difference between this mindset and the Leader's Mind. He said, "Son, respect is earned and never given; therefore, in order to get respect you have to give it." The Leader understands that authority carries with it responsibility, not respect. The respect of your team comes from earning their respect. So how do we do that?

Well the here are some ideas about respect from great Leaders throughout history:

"Treat your [team] as you would your own beloved [children]. And they will follow you into the deepest valley." -- General Sun Tzu, *The Art of War*

"People don't care how much you know until they know how much you care." -- Dale Carnegie, author of *How to Win Friends and Influence People*

"People will forget what you say, and they will forget what you do, but they will never forget how you make them feel." -- Dr. Maya Angelou

Shift Key 1: Appreciating the importance of your team's respect, not just their obedience, is one of the key components to developing the Leader's Mind.

The Leader vs. the Follower/The Mission vs. the Team

Similar to the previous point about authority, the Manager's Mind is focused on the role of the Leader from an authority and responsibility perspective. The problem is such a focus is too narrow. It doesn't understand the fact that the Leader only exists because there are followers for them to lead.

As Derek Sivers discussed in his TED talk entitled, "How to Start a Movement," until a leader has a follower, he is just a crazy person. The followers are what give the Leader true authority and responsibility. They are what give the mission its meaning. This is a difficult concept for many managers to grasp, especially since they feel that people are hired to do a job and they should do it. To embrace the reality that the people you lead truly have the power is incongruent with the lessons of Executive Leadership. Furthermore, to be able to realize that our true responsibility as Leaders is to take care of the people you were placed in charge of. Understanding this and accepting it takes maturity.

Shift Key #2: The Leader's Mind keeps the focus of their efforts on giving more and more power away.

Team vs. Mission

This is also why the Leader's Mind is constantly focused on the Team rather than the Mission. To be clear, the Empowering Leader is concerned with the mission being accomplished; that is simply not her focus. The Empowering Leader understands the critical truth that if the team is taken care of, the mission will get accomplished if it is at all possible and even sometimes when it is impossible.

Therefore, the Leader's Mind is focused on ensuring that the Team is capable of accomplishing the mission. The Leader's Mind looks for obstacles in the system or infrastructure that may prevent the team from performing in the way that they are capable. The Leader's Mind is always looking for a way to take care of the team. This is the focus of the Leader's Mind.

Shift Key #3: Take care of the team to accomplish the mission.

Taking our example from earlier, if my fellow lieutenant had been using a Leader's Mind, he would have devised a plan that both accomplished the mission and took care of the team. Because he was solely focused on the mission (and this focus was based largely on his fear of getting himself in trouble by not accomplishing the mission. We will discuss this in Chapter 5), he lost the trust and the respect of the platoon, many for the entirety of the six months that we trained together. Instead of focusing on the minor details of what everyone must be doing, the Empowering Leader is focused on ensuring that everyone has the support and the encouragement they need to perform at their best and then trusts them to do so. The Empowering Leader is determined to set their team up for success while also preparing them to learn from their mistakes along the way.

***

Ultimately, when you develop the Leader's Mind you understand that the enterprise is not about you. It is about the Team. It's about their experiences, their growth, their empowerment. The Empowering Leader understands and is secure in the knowledge that they have the ability to do the work. But, more importantly, the Empowering Leader understands that doing the work is no longer his responsibility. That is why the team is there.

The Leader's Mind comprehends on the deepest level that the Leader's job is building their team, earning their respect, developing their trust, and cultivating their abilities. The Empowering Leader understands that if they do their job right, their people will no longer need them, and that is a good thing. The goal is to work themselves out of a job. Empowering Leaders don't want to be the focus. They understand that their goal is to eventually be unnecessary. The Leader's Mind embodies the idea discussed in this quote by the Taoist sage Lao Tzu discussing leadership:

"A leader is best when people barely know he exists, when his work is done, his aim fulfilled, they will say: We did it ourselves!" –Lao Tzu

In order to successfully make the transition from an Executing Leader to Empowering Leader to Legacy Leader, it is imperative that you fully grasp this concept of the continuum of leadership for both you and those you lead. By understanding your role on this continuum, you can better embrace your purpose as a leader. Many people get stuck in the Executing Leader role because they don't fully embrace their need to grow from Do-er to Master. They never learn to accept the fact that to be a great helper/leader, you must become a master of receiving help as well. For so long they have found their worth in what they do, what they could accomplish without help. It's easy to get stuck and plateau and not realize that, in order to expand, you need others.

However, embracing the purpose of this continuum and its impact on your role as a leader is the solution to being stuck. The purpose of The Leader's Way, the purpose of the leadership in general, is to make the world a better place by helping others to manifest the greatness that lies within them and then empowering them to do the same for others. This is how you develop a Leadership Legacy worth remembering. Embracing this purpose will allow you do much more than just increasing the productivity of your people or getting your employees to do their jobs without constant oversight. Embracing your role as an Empowering Leader and ultimately a Legacy Leader is how you become the type of leader that gets the best effort out of your people on every project, that creates other leaders, the type of leader that changes the world.

Think back to the great coaches or other leaders of history. No one cares what type of basketball player Phil Jackson was, what type of football player Vince Lombardi was, or what type of engineer Steve Jobs was. They don't have highlight reels of their individual accomplishments (even though they were all pretty good). What they are remembered for is the fact that they were able to empower a group of people to manifest their greatness and, because of that, amazing things happened. This first step, transitioning to Empowering Leadership, is all about the results that you help others to produce. Your ability to get more out of them than they even knew was in them.

***

Embedded throughout this discussion will be references to Legacy Leadership. I want to be transparent with you here. Though this book and this step of your journey is about becoming an Empowering Leader, the true purpose of this path is to ensure that you are not just helping your people to produce greatness today but that you are empowering them to produce greatness when you are gone.

One of the core principles of my Legacy Empowerment Academy is in its name, Legacy. And it comes from this verse in Proverbs which says, "The wise person leaves an inheritance [legacy] to their children's children." Proverbs 13:22.

Now, here's the good news: If you can embrace this purpose and make it your passion, you will leave a legacy of leadership wherever you go. As we move forward to discuss the Leader's

Toolkit (and how your Mindset is the determining factor in whether you can use the tools effectively), what you will see is that your main job is to simply support and facilitate the journey of your team along this continuum, to help. This is done by opening up the Leader's Heart that you have cultivated during your time as an Executive Leader and letting them know how much you care.

As we move onto the Leader's Toolkit, I want to give you one maxim that should guide you as you read through the rest of the strategies we will discuss. It is this: Empowering Leadership is about fidelity to core values while at the same time being committed to progress and innovation. (For more on this balance, see *Built to Last* by Jim Collins). Those core values are Interdependence, Empowerment, and Growth. Remembering this will make everything else much easier to implement.

The rest of this book is broken up into the three parts of the toolkit: Vision; Communication and Strategy; and Tactics, Techniques, and Procedures (TTPs). The sections dealing with Vision are there to focus you on getting clear on where you are trying to lead your team. Until you know where you are going, the how and even the why don't really matter. Next, we move into the strategy sections. These will help you to communicate and gather support for your Vision. This is necessary if you are going to change the way your team performs and achieve the goals that you have for yourself: getting them to take more initiative, reducing your stress, and inspiring their best. Finally, we will discuss the TTPs. These are specific measures that you will use to implement your strategy and to create the type of environment that you need for your people to perform at their best.

SECTION 1: VISION

Chapter 4: Begin with the End In Mind

"Setting Goals is the First Step in turning the invisible into the visible" -- Tony Robbins

(E)MPOWER: Examine and Evaluate Your Expectations

Now, we begin our discussion about the tools needed to excel at being an Empowering Leader. These tools will help you become the type of leader that brings out the best work in everyone who works with you. More importantly, these tools will allow you to be the type of leader that creates other leaders. At all times during this discussion, keep at the forefront of your thoughts the core values of an Empowering Leader: Empowerment and Growth. Everything that we focus on will be designed to maximize those values. But first, a word of caution...

Trust the Process

When I was becoming certified as a Gracie Jiu Jitsu Instructor, one of the things that my teachers Ryron and Rener Gracie used to say to us all the time was "trust the process." They taught us about how important it was for us as instructors not to try to teach everything we know about Jiu Jitsu to our students in their first lesson or in their first ten lessons. They taught us that if we trust the process, in six months to a year we would have students who could defend themselves, and, more importantly, these students would own that knowledge forever. They understood that, as teachers with Leader's Hearts, we had the desire to help and to make a difference. They also understood that if we used the Manager's Mindset, we would damage our relationships with our students and possibly ruin a truly life-changing experience.

What they told us then, and what I am telling you now, is that if you truly want to make a difference, if you truly want to help your team reach their potential, if you truly want your team to do their jobs so that you can focus on the things that you should be focusing on, then you have to trust the process. You must remember that though it may take a bit longer than you think it should, your team will get there. And here is the counterintuitive part: Once you let go of trying to do it for them, you will be amazed at how quickly they begin to learn and improve.

So how do you get to the point where you can let go? One of the things that we will focus on will be to set up processes and systems that turn potential into reality. Additionally, you will focus on optimizing your people's strengths rather than fixing their weaknesses.

It has often been said that as a leader you need to help your people to strengthen their weaknesses, and this is true. However, the purpose and manner in which we do so can often be the difference between success and failure, between empowerment and condescension. Many leaders focus on pointing out the weak points of their team in hopes that the team will correct their deficiencies. Or they set up situations that test them in areas that they are weak, trying to make them stronger. Some even set up scenarios for the team to fail in hopes that their failure will impress upon them the importance of improving and motivate them to do so. However, these tactics normally backfire.

The premise is all wrong. Operating from a weakness centered mindset is working from the perspective that a) your team doesn't know where they are weak and b) they could get better if they just worked harder. Education, Psychology, and Child Development professionals have been exclaiming the powers of positive reinforcement for decades, and it is important that you understand that positive reinforcement starts with how you set up your systems and processes. We will discuss more about the science behind this position in the Reward Your Team chapter. For now, I want you to consider this question:

Have you truly Developed Reasonable Expectations that set your team up for success rather than failure?

One of the pitfalls you may face when Leading in Manager or Supervisor mode is allowing your laser-like focus on your objectives to cause you to develop unreasonable expectations. This is problematic but understandable. It stems from the fact that we get so used to being an executor, a Do-er. You get your mission, and you execute. Whatever obstacles are necessary to overcome, you overcome them. This has become so much of your identity and routine that you forget to even think about whether the objective is reasonable.

As a leader, this can be disastrous. It is very easy to allow these objectives to drive everything and to create pressure that is unnecessary and counterproductive. Oftentimes, this will lead you to request unreasonable things from your team in order to meet these objectives. In turn, you lose the very respect and the trust you need to lead your team before the mission even begins.

The Empowering Leader understands that respect and trust are key to the success of the team. He also understands that having a positive outlook for the future is important to conveying the right message to your team about your belief in them. Therefore, the first thing that you want to do as an Empowering Leader when given a task, even before you agree to accept it, is to ensure your expectations of your team are reasonable. You want to make sure that you are not allowing yourself to sabotage your endeavor before it even begins. As you gain proficiency at this, your mind will become more open to the myriad ways you can deal with a challenge. You will also begin to see how you can overcome any obstacle with your team once you have a handle on the situation. Simply by developing the proper expectations from the outset, you will reduce stress, increase trust, and ultimately be able to accomplish more than you originally thought possible.

***

There are three prerequisite steps to being able to ensure your expectations are reasonable. These are:

1. Examine, aka Take Inventory;
2. Evaluate, aka Assess Capabilities and Limitations; and
3. Optimize your Strengths and Mitigate your Weaknesses by Developing Reasonable Long- and Short-Term Goals aka Expectations

One of my mentors, Dean Graziosi, often says the following, "People will overestimate what they can do in one year and underestimate what they can do in five." This is especially true of leaders who are new to their teams. We often look at their capabilities and assume that, since they are capable, they will be performing at their capacity relatively quickly. When we realize that they are not performing at this level and that they are not going to get there quickly, it is easy to get discouraged about the potential of your team to reach its greatness. It's OK, we all have to go through this phase so that we can truly understand and trust the process.

Here is a great point to take us back to grade school. Science class to be exact. A lesson regarding inertia and the difference between potential energy and kinetic energy. Kinetic energy is the energy of motion, the energy of work. Potential energy is the energy stored in an object which is at rest. We can think of it as latent or dormant energy. Inertia is the tendency of a thing at rest to stay at rest. In order to convert Potential Energy to Kinetic Energy there has to be some stimulus that breaks the inertia of that resting state. Some outside force must serve as a catalyst and that force has to be enough to get the resting object moving. The internal potential energy is not activated until that external force acts on it. This is key.

Too often, as leaders, we see people who have great potential and expect that realizing that potential is an easy endeavor. We also expect them to make it happen and are disappointed if they don't. However, science tells us that it is not their responsibility, but rather it is ours. The greatest amount of energy in the process of going from potential to reality is the energy needed to overcome inertia. After that, it's literally coasting downhill. Therefore, in the next section of the book, we look at how to design your communication and personnel placement strategies in a way that specializes in overcoming this inertia and ultimately helps your team reach their fullest potential.

***

So what do I mean when I say "Examine your Expectations, aka Take Inventory?" I mean you need to get to really know your team. So often, as leaders, we are given a team without getting a chance to pick them. Therefore, unless you were part of the hiring/interview committee, the only chance you get to know your team members is after they are already on your team. Maybe you get an initial interview with them and then you get to speak with them during their reviews. Other than those formal interactions, many leaders rarely have the time to socialize with subordinates and get to know them in more informal settings. In many places, it is actually frowned upon. Because of this, many leaders never truly get to understand their people.

This is the cause of many of our unreasonable expectations. We make assumptions about our people without ever really examining whether those assumptions are accurate. Then we create expectations based on those assumptions. When our people fail to live up to those expectations, we are disappointed and begin to lose faith in their ability to live up to the potential that we saw in them. Taking inventory solves this problem.

One of the things that stuck with me from my time training for and working as a teacher was the importance of getting to know who your students really were. It was so important to know more than who they were in your presence. Over and over, we were taught about how important it was to know where they lived, what their families were like, what type of music they listened to, what sports they liked, etc.

With my own students, I found this to be so true. To be a good teacher, I had to truly understand my students, to see the world as they saw it. And they had to know that I cared about more than just what they could do. They had to know that I cared about who they were and who they were trying to become. By learning about their family histories and their music preferences, I got to know more about how they saw the world and what motivated them to be their best. I also got to earn their trust. These things influenced the expectations that I had for them and helped me to take them much farther than they thought was possible.

***

The good news is that it is not as hard as it sounds to get this information about those that you lead, and it can actually be a very enlightening and endearing experience. It is also the key to Empowering Leadership. It is imperative that you have a broad understanding of the people on your team if you are going to help them become the best version of themselves.

There are many ways to go about this. One of the more effective and efficient ways is to have your team do personality profiles. There are many to choose from Enneagrams, Myers Briggs, Strength Finder 2.0, DISC, etc. Which method you choose is not as important as understanding what it will tell you and how to use that information. To ensure that you fully understand the assessment and how it works, I recommend that you begin by taking it for yourself and fully reviewing your results.

This analysis will give you very insightful information about yourself as a leader. You can then have your team take the profiles that you took so that you can gain insight into your team's strengths and weaknesses as well as compatibilities and work styles. It will also help you to understand how to relate to your team members as individuals, and as a team, in a way that caters toward their strengths. This information is invaluable as you begin to do the next step and assess the capabilities and limitations of your team.

***

Once you have taken an inventory of your team, you are better equipped to truly evaluate your expectations and develop reasonable long-term and short-term expectations for your team. Back when I was coaching high school and middle school basketball, I often had teams where this was the first year my players were playing organized ball. When we faced off against teams where the players obviously played summer league ball and AAU ball, it would have been foolish for me to have the expectation that my team win those games. Of course, I could still hope that we win those games, but if I put that expectation on my team, they would have felt that pressure to be way better than they were.

There is a difference between believing they can and believing they should. Had I believed that since they were capable then they should win and treated them that way, I would have created a lose/lose situation. Either I immediately lose trust with them because I would be expecting them to do something that they were in no way prepared for, or they believe me and then continually feel like failures when they don't reach the unrealistic expectation. Either way, I am not leading them towards their greatness. Instead, you use the information you have about your team to figure out the places where your team can be successful and focus on those areas.

Using our previous example, I taught all of my teams how to break the press as one of the first things we did in practice. We drilled it, and they got good at it. If we were playing a team that pressed, every time they would press, we would break it. We might not score at the other end because we still had work to do on shooting and scoring (much more difficult than breaking a press). However, my team would feel the joy of accomplishment in breaking it. Similarly, I would celebrate them breaking the press, and they would know that they impressed me because they had met the expectation that I set for them. This ensured that they would continue these positive behaviors that had gotten us to this point. See Chapter 11 for more discussion on the Power of Positive Reinforcement.

I developed these beneficial expectations because I evaluated whether my expectations were reasonable in relation to our strengths and weaknesses at the moment. Once I knew they were reasonable, then I set about putting all of our focus on meeting them. The tool that we will discuss next will allow you to do the same. It is called a SWOT Analysis. You will use this tool at various points of your implementation of the EMPOWER Method to ensure that you develop and maintain reasonable and beneficial expectations for your team.

The SWOT Analysis

SWOT is an acronym that stands for: Strengths, Weaknesses, Opportunities, and Threats. The purpose of this analysis is to give the leader an appropriate view of the battlespace or playing field so as to allow them to make informed decisions about next steps. For the Empowering Leader, performing a SWOT analysis allows you to ensure that you are, at all times, setting your team up for success.

To perform a SWOT Analysis is relatively easy, and I recommend that you do one on yourself first to get the process down. Once you have the hang of it, it will be easy for you to apply it to your team. The rest of this section relates to how you apply it to your team.

> Complete your Personal SWOT Analysis Worksheet NOW!!!!
>
> Go to this link: https://www.facebook.com/groups/LegacyLeaders2018/ and join my #LegacyLeaders.
>
> As a thank you for helping me to reach my goal of developing 1 million #LegacyLeaders in the next 10 years, I have created a free seven-part video series that outlines the principles of Empowering Leadership and made it available to all of my #LegacyLeaders. I have also included a number of useful tools to help you along your Leadership Journey, including a Personal SWOT Analysis Exercise.
>
> Go on over to https://www.facebook.com/groups/LegacyLeaders2018 to get access.

(S)trengths

The first step of your SWOT Analysis is to list all of the strengths of your team. You can do this individually, or you can group people together depending on how your team functions. If your team is broken up into smaller teams, you might want to begin by listing the strengths of each of those teams collectively.

Ultimately, however, you want to drill this down so that you have a unique skill set and role for each person on your team. You want each person to have their thing – the skill/task that they are the go-to person for on the team.

You want to look at all the areas where your team is better than average and particularly places where your team can be the best at a particular thing, the places where your team is uniquely qualified to compete. Your goal is to look at all the things that your team excels at. You can use the information that you got from your personality assessments as a starting place, and then, you can also look to job performance and other evaluative measures to give you more information.

(W)eaknesses

Next, you want to take a critical look at your team and the places where they are weak. This has sometimes been euphemized to be called places where they have room for improvement; however, for the purposes of this analysis, we don't want to look at it like that. When you actually address these areas with your team then, yes, we can use the nice language and focus on the positive. However, that is because at the time that we let them know about our perception of their weaknesses. The purpose will be for building and improving. When we discuss long term planning, you will revisit these areas and treat them like the more traditional "room for improvement" paradigm.

But here, for our purposes of evaluating our expectations, you want to look to these weak areas as vulnerabilities to the overall enterprise. These are areas where your team is lacking and below average in their capabilities. The point here is that when you are evaluating your expectations you are looking at a goal with a specific timeline and purpose (see Chapter 6 for more discussion of SMART goals). Because our expectations are goal-centric, it is imperative in this analysis that you look at the realities of the present, not what can possibly change in the future. The importance of this perspective is crucial to our work when we begin to look at the Threats analysis.

(O)pportunities

At this stage of your analysis, you want to project into the future, both the near future and the distant future. Based on your strengths, what are the types of tasks, projects, and other opportunities that, in the present and the future, you will be able, to take advantage of if they come your way? These are the things that when they come to your team you immediately know, "We can do this." These are the projects that you hope for, that you prepare for, that you know that you are going to rock. These are the tasks where you have the highest of expectations for your team because you know that they are not only capable of accomplishing them but knocking them out of the park because these opportunities play to their strengths.

I want to be clear: You MUST be proactive about your opportunity analysis. It is possibly the most important analysis to maintaining your passion and joy as a leader. By doing this analysis well, you can work hard on the front end to ensure that your team picks up more of these opportunities. You can use your influence with your superiors/customers to get the specifications tailored to the benefit of your team. You can set your team up for success as their advocate. Similarly, this is the analysis that gives you hope for the future with your team. Lastly, it helps to clarify your personnel decisions going forward. If you have a need that isn't filled, it is here that you can determine with laser accuracy who you need to hire and how that hire will be of benefit to the team.

As previously discussed, one of the primary tools of a leader is vision: the ability to see things that others might not see. Because of your certainty about your team's strengths, your vision and your optimism for the future are increased. That hope is then communicated to your team in all that you do with them and for them. It's what makes them know you care and believe in them. That belief is what makes them trust you and believe in your belief in them, even when they may doubt themselves. This analysis is crucial to developing these virtues in your team and to developing your team into leaders. The information from the opportunity analysis will help you hone your aspirational visions for your team and will help you gain the most from a social capital perspective with your team.

(T)hreats

The threat analysis is possibly the most difficult to perform and explain since it is a really nuanced concept. Explaining it is made even more difficult by our cultural and evolutionary programming regarding threats. We have been taught to look at threats as negative things and that we should eliminate them. However, the operating from the position that we can eliminate threats creates an unreasonable expectation. As we have just reviewed, there will always be areas where your team is relatively weaker and areas where they are relatively stronger. In any area where there is weakness, there will always be the threat of that weakness hampering your ability to take advantage of an opportunity. Therefore, instead of endeavoring to eliminate threats, we are going to focus on determining how we can minimize them and minimize their impact on our operations. By doing so, we will turn them into opportunities for growth.

So how do we analyze a threat for the opportunities it affords us? Very carefully. In the Weaknesses section above, I told you that our perspective on weaknesses would be very important in this section, and this is why: Weaknesses (and Strengths for that matter) are relative measures of ability. Their only importance is in relation to how they affect our ability to take advantage of opportunities. Our weaknesses being the places where we have the least relative advantage means that they are the places where we must mitigate the most in our planning regarding our opportunities.

In the Marine Corps, threat (the life or death kind) was a common issue that we had to deal with as officers. We were trained to understand our greatest weakness (the fact that humans die if they get shot or blown up) was a threat to our success. Considering that war is an enterprise that is literally about life and death, training for it is a tricky endeavor. As an officer, you are constantly trying to prepare your troops for the reality of the situation, while at the same time, trying to keep them safe in training. This training however, cannot be done in such a way as to eliminate all risk. To do so would make the training ineffective and would create an unreasonable expectation for the leader and the troops. The only way to truly learn how to shoot a rifle or to maneuver as a fire-team in a live fire situation is to do it.

Because of this dilemma, the Marine Corps created the Operational Risk Management process to minimize the threat. In this process, leaders look at the purpose of the tasks, evaluate the risks that are inherent to the goal, think of ways to mitigate the risks, implement those mitigation procedures, and then evaluate whether the purpose of the mission makes the mitigated risk worth taking.

Looking at risk/threats the way the Marine Corps does is very helpful to understanding this step of your SWOT analysis. We must also remember that threats are always potential in nature. They are not guaranteed, just potential outcomes. So we will look at ways to mitigate their occurrence. We can do this in both the short term and the long term. And the good part about handling them in this way is that by doing so we can also use them to create more opportunities for growth.

For example, if your team has a problem in turning things in on time, that is a weakness relative to the teams that meet their deadlines. The ways that this can affect your team's opportunities are many, but the main one is that missing deadlines can result in penalties and/or damages and possibly even the loss of business. Therefore, the most important thing is to recognize that your team has this weakness. The next thing is to mitigate the risk of this weakness impacting your opportunity.

What that looks like in practice is what we call in the Marine Corps, "Gunny Time." This comes from the fact that young people (who make up the majority of the Marine Corps) are notorious for forgetting things and showing up late. Therefore, to mitigate for those weaknesses and their ability to interfere with the mission, if the report time for an event is 8:00 in the morning, the Gunnery Sergeant (a high-ranking enlisted official with usually fifteen or more years in the service) will generally mandate that everyone of a lower rank be there fifteen minutes or more prior to the event. This becomes the new report time. Generally, those down the line are not even aware of the true start time as only the "Gunny Time" is reported. Now, if anyone is late or unprepared, the team has 15 minutes to fix whatever the problem was.

This mitigates for the short-term; however, it is not a permanent solution. That is why the threats analysis is also a section to develop opportunities for growth in the future. In this case, you might begin planning to get your people time-management training in the not too distant future, with the expectation that they will be able to improve their ability to be more time conscious relative to others over time.

Ultimately, we must begin to see that threats are really just opportunities in disguise. By mitigating for threats, we are able to improve our ability as leaders to think through challenges before we have to face them. Similarly, by dealing with them in this mitigated way when they happen, our team is better because we are able to still be successful even when things don't go exactly the way we wanted them to. Lastly, we create the space that we need to make lasting change in them by ensuring that the urgency of the threat is mitigated. This allows us to actually transform our people's weaknesses rather than just point them out and leave the heavy lifting to them. By using our threats to create opportunities in the present and the future, we reduce the stress to be better now. This allows us as leaders to have more reasonable expectations for our people while at the same time maintaining our hope for their potential. This gains us their respect and their trust in the long-run and is very important to our ability to get them to manifest their greatness.

***

By looking at your team through the lens of your SWOT analysis, you are better able to evaluate and assess what they are capable of and what their limitations are. You are also more prepared to help them seize the opportunities they are ready for and mitigate against the threats to their performance. Lastly, you are better able to structure your systems and your processes to absorb the areas where you need to grow as a team in the short term. This, in turn, will give you the time that you need to actually improve in those areas.

By Taking Inventory and Evaluating Your Capabilities and Limitations, you set the proper conditions for you to accurately assess your team and develop reasonable expectations of their performance in the short term and over the long haul. This is the first step of leading your team to their potential greatness. The expectations you set are the foundation for everything going forward. Once you have reasonable expectations of your team, you will be better prepared to lead them and, ultimately, to prepare them to lead themselves and others. Examining and Evaluating your expectations and, more importantly, having reasonable expectations of what your team can do in the present is crucial to your ability to project hope, faith, and trust in them to be better in the future.

As an Empowering Leader, it is important that you are consciously and unconsciously believing in your team and the process of your leadership. This is because as the leader, you are generally the first source of belief that your people have that they can be more than they are. We will discuss in more detail the conscious and unconscious communication cues you give your team in the next chapter. For now, just know that your expectations of your team will filter into everything else you do. Therefore, it is imperative that before you try to lead them anywhere, you evaluate your expectations of their performance and ensure that you are setting them up for success.

Chapter 5: Matrix Moments

"It is not the spoon that bends, it is you!"–scene from the movie, "The Matrix"

E(M)POWER: Measure Expectations

In the movie The Matrix, the whole plot is centered around how the heroes can manipulate, bend, and even break the rules of reality because of the fact that the world that they are living in is a construct; it is a virtual reality. In one of the scenes in the movie Neo, the main hero character, is in an apartment waiting to speak with the Oracle. The apartment is really a type of sanctuary for gifted children whom the Oracle is raising and helping to understand and develop their abilities.

The focal point of this scene comes when Neo watches a child bend a spoon with the power of his mind. As Neo discusses how to do it with the boy, the child drops a little nugget of wisdom that forms the foundation for this chapter – hence, Matrix Moments. In the scene, the child explains, "Do not try and bend the spoon. That's impossible. Instead, only try to realize the truth... There is no spoon. Then you'll see that it is not the spoon that bends. It is only yourself."

This is the secret truth of leadership:

There is no spoon!

Without getting too metaphysical here, the point to take away from this is that as the Leader, you determine what success is for your team. You control whether your team succeeds or fails because you define success and failure. Period!!!

That may or may not be linked to your own success. Whether it is or not is irrelevant. The point is that, for your team, they only have the reality that you give them. They only have the success targets that you give them. Therefore, however you define success is what will determine whether they feel successful or not, whether they are successful or not.

Realize this truth! There is no authoritative definition of success. It is whatever you as the leader determine for your team. Therefore, in continuing with our work from the last chapter, as an Empowering Leader, it is imperative that at all times you define success in such a way that you cater to your team's strengths and mitigate their weaknesses. Ultimately, your goal is that your definition of success for your team does three things:

- Sets them up for success;
- Focuses on their strengths, and
- Gets your team excited about the challenge

Setting Your Team Up for Success:
Key #1: Rethink How You Define Success to Your Team

One key difference that must be discussed is the difference between setting your team up for success and lowering your standards for excellence. You can prepare your team for success and create an environment for them to be successful without lowering your standards for excellence. Your team will rise to meet your standards as the leader, however high or low they may be. Similarly, your team will never try to do great things if they don't believe... that you believe... that they can be successful. It is important to remember, however, that your team may not be able to achieve your ultimate idea of excellence in their current state. And if you base their success or failure on their ability to achieve that ultimate idea, you will never be able to get the best out of your team.

    The conventional wisdom on performance is that people don't try hard because they are lazy or have low standards. I do not believe this is normally the case. I believe that people don't try hard when they don't believe they can be successful and/or when they don't believe that they are expected to be successful. This is for two reasons: 1) Because of our cultural conditioning, the pain of trying and failing is tremendous, and it is therefore something we all try to avoid and 2) because you have nothing to prove and no one to impress if your leader doesn't believe in you anyway.

Note - It is the rare person that is willing to work hard to prove people wrong. These people are the exception rather than the rule. Usually, lack of belief doesn't challenge people; it just confirms that impressing those people is not worth the time. It inspires apathy not struggle.

    If you want your team to accomplish great things, you have to nurture their belief in themselves at all times throughout this process. Similarly, your team will pick up on your belief in their ability to be successful from your verbal and non-verbal cues, from your conscious and your unconscious communication with them.

As an Empowering Leader, you have to always be on guard for how you are communicating to your team and how you are thinking about their potential for success. This gets easier when you have the systems and processes in place that we discuss later in the book. But, it is important for me to bring your attention to it here because your people will rise to meet your true expectations for them, not just the ones you espouse in your discussions with them. So when you are having doubts about their potential or the outcome of the project, make sure that you are aware of this and that you work to deal with that personally (see Step 1) before you ever interact with them.

Key #2: Measurement is Critical

This is another one of the key leadership themes that are interwoven throughout all of the steps on the path to becoming an Empowering Leader. Here, I want to introduce you to the concept of SMART goal setting and discuss how critical having metrics is to measuring your team's expectations.

SMART is an acronym that stands for:

- Specific
- Measurable
- Assignable/Achievable
- Relevant

- Timebound

By using this method of setting goals your team is able to easily understand what you expect them to achieve. Additionally, as we will discuss throughout the rest of the EMPOWER Method, the SMART strategy will enable them to determine whether they have achieved it. Measurement is critical to everything that you are going to do going forward because it allows your team to view their work the way that you do. Just like standard units of measurement transformed global commerce and science, standard, objective, and measurable evaluation methods will transform your team from being reliant on you to determine whether they are doing a good job to being able to do it for themselves.

How does one develop these measurements? By becoming clear on their visions. Many leaders struggle with getting their teams to accomplish their goals because they do not have clarity on what they need their teams to do. Therefore, they cannot give their team the proper frameworks to determine, on their own, whether they have accomplished their objectives. This, in turn, increases the amount of time and effort it takes to manage the team and supervise their work. It also leaves a team dependent upon supervisory approval for validation of their work. This is inherently less efficient and less effective because, no matter how talented, the leader is only one person and can't be everywhere at once. Lack of clarity and the resulting lack of objective measurement methods is the reason that many leaders feel like they are doing everyone else's job as well as their own. This lack of clarity severely limits a leader's ability to delegate effectively.

We will discuss this in depth when we discuss Specificity in next the chapter on the Principles of Proper Delegation. For now, just know that the method that you use set and communicate goals is important not only for your team but for you as well. When you know what you want from your team and you know how to measure their performance, it relieves stress from you during the process. Similarly, when you know that your team understands what you want, you have more faith that they will be able to accomplish the task, and you are more comfortable holding them accountable.

The calm reassurance that is the result of this knowledge will be transmitted to your team via your demeanor and your language. They will know that you believe in them, that you trust them, and that you trust in the mission you have set before them. In turn they will trust you more than any amount of authority that's bestowed in your title. And this trust will have been earned, even before you give them a job to do.

This is the secret to getting the best out of your team on every project. You must set yourself up to be able trust them and the process. By doing this, by setting reasonable expectations for yourself and defining success in a way that makes it almost impossible for them to fail, you will have more comfort believing in them (and not that Pollyanna-ish, rose colored glasses belief... No, I'm talking about really believing in them). This belief is something they will feel without you even verbalizing it, and they will reciprocate it.

Key #3: Align Your Methods to Your Purpose

Another myth of leadership is that in order for a goal to be worthwhile then it has to be a tremendous struggle to reach it. I disagree. When we actually look at those who succeed and excel in any given area, the percentage of those that succeed despite tremendous struggle is actually very small. Some struggle is OK, but past a certain point, it will have a diminishing return and can even exponentially increase the likelihood of catastrophic failure.

For example, in the martial arts, for the vast majority of those that begin to study, the goal is to learn to defend oneself. Similarly, the goal of most martial arts instructors is to teach people how to defend themselves. The two seem congruent on the surface. The student goes to class with the purpose of learning self-defense, and the teacher teaches with the purpose of helping the student learn to defend themselves. Looks like we have alignment, just like most teams after a quarterly review or annual meeting. So, let's look at how methods being misaligned throws the whole thing off the rails.

In most martial arts, it generally takes between six and twelve months, and some even up to ten years, before one is deemed to be qualified to defend themselves against your average attacker (assuming a standard training week of two to three classes per week). Conversely, the industry standard for students is that 90% quit before they have been training for 6 months. Why the disconnect? If the students and the teachers are aligned in their purpose, what is causing 90% of students to leave the practice before accomplishing their objective? The answer: Methods are not aligned with purpose!

Most martial arts training is based on the reality that in order to be able to defend oneself, you must develop certain foundational attributes: grit, perseverance, toughness, and strength. Because these are actual necessities that must be developed, many martial arts schools focus heavily on developing these during that first six months. Their objective is to lay a good foundation. There is a lot of conditioning work and exercises that test one's commitment to their goal. For the student it generally feels as if the instructor is determining whether they have the mettle for the training in this first six months. And not surprisingly, most people do not pass the test. Hence, the 90% departure rate.

As we have discussed, I am a Gracie Jiu Jitsu Certified Instructor; however, I have studied a number of martial arts, and I can attest to this incongruence personally. I have seen so many people leave over the nearly twenty years I have been practicing. This was even the case with my current instructors for many years. Like in other martial arts, in Gracie Jiu Jitsu, attaining self-defense proficiency generally takes about six months to a year for the average student. And like most arts, for many years, the number of students leaving the practice was tracking the industry standard. Only about 10 % of students would stay longer than six months.

For a long time, the belief was that people just couldn't take the training. They wanted it easy... Their weakness was the problem. Then in the early 2000s, my instructors began to question this reasoning. They began to look at the incongruence between the aligned interests at the beginning and the outcomes of the training methods. They looked at the fact that the reason that the people were coming in the first place was that they were not comfortable in situations where they were being dominated and overpowered. The people already realized before they walked through the door that they didn't have what it took to defend themselves. That's why they joined a team and found a teacher. And they began to look at their methods more closely.

The Gracies realized that their methods were not aligned to their purpose. They realized that if they were going to help people by teaching them to defend themselves, then they needed to figure out a way to get people to stay in the system long enough to actually benefit from the training (six months to a year). This was especially important to the Gracies because their mission was to serve those that needed self-defense the most–the small, the weak, the unathletic and uncoordinated, the people most likely to be bullied and taken advantage of by those more powerful than them.

In the nearly 20 years since they made the switch, they have had more people try and stick with Jiu Jitsu than ever before. And since 2009, they have certified instructors and opened up over 120 academies around the world. Consequently, they have students who would never have made it in the old days developing a love for the art and working all the way to Black Belt. This is the paradigm under which I became an instructor, and it has greatly influenced my understanding of leadership and the need to align our methods with our long-term purpose and our values.

Side note: One of my proudest achievements is that one of my students who came to me after having given up on Jiu Jitsu because of this very issue (she was a 120-pound woman who didn't like getting thrown around by the guys and not really feeling like she was learning) is one of those helped by the alignment of methods and purpose. She began with a women's self-defense class that I was teaching. She joined, excelled, and went on to join the co-ed class. She then earned her blue belt.

She is now an instructor in the co-ed class, has led other women to join, and routinely shows the young men who come to our school full of energy and bravado that she is more than capable of defending herself. In the time since I moved away, she and another one of my students have kept the self-defense programs going. She is also running the women's self-defense program that she started in and carrying on that dream. She has become a Leader who is creating other Leaders.

Ultimately, you must always keep in mind your short- and long-term objectives when you are creating your systems and processes and when you are defining success for your team. You must make sure that they are aligned. Being clear about what your goal is and knowing how to measure success is key to this alignment. It is not just what you measure or how you measure; it is also how much what you measure is aligned with the purpose of your leadership. An Empowering Leader ensures that their expectations, their systems, and their processes provide the greatest chance for the success of their team. Again, that is the overall purpose of the Leader, the success of your team.

***

And that brings us back to the spoon. I want to be clear here: your team will struggle to improve and to accomplish great things. But how they perceive that struggle is critical to their overall success and to the lessons that they learn about their accomplishments on the way to becoming Leaders themselves.

You see, the truth about struggle is that it is largely a relative idea based on our perception of ourselves in relation to external reference points. And this perception of how well we are doing in relation to our peers or some preconceived notion of success impacts our performance. What this means is that people who believe they are expected to do well and believe that they are doing well will often continue to do well. This is why your congruent communication with your team is so important.

On the same note, people that believe that they are struggling and that they shouldn't be struggling will generally continue to struggle and perform at a level lower than they are capable of. Malcolm Gladwell discusses this in his book, *David and Goliath*. In Chapter 3, he tells the story of Caroline Sacks, a brilliant girl who dreamed of being a scientist until she struggled in organic chemistry as a student at Brown. Gladwell uses her story to explain how people's perception of their relative position has a tremendous influence on their activities, their development of grit, and ultimately their outcomes. In Caroline's case, while she was brilliant and in the top 99% of students in Organic Chemistry as compared to all students in the country, she felt like she was stupid and incompetent when compared to her fellow classmates at Brown. This led her to abandon her dream of being a scientist. She still graduated, but she definitely did not reach potential.

This is termed relative deprivation. Gladwell explains this concept in relation to the educational phenomena known as the Big Fish Little Pond Effect. This happens to students who come from schools where they are at the top of their class and rarely struggle. When they move to elite institutions where everyone is used to being in the top of their class, they tend to experience struggle for the first time. This is a traumatic experience for them because, though they may have gotten a couple points off or struggled to get things done, they have never received a B or lower. They have never been in the middle of the class. Hence: relative deprivation.

The higher the bar is set to get into an institution, the worse students feel about their academic abilities and the more they feel that the other students around them are more qualified and capable than they are. Students who would be in the top tier of their class at a good school can easily fall to the bottom of their class at an elite school. And this fall wreaks havoc on their perception of their worth.

Many believe that this is because of their lack of being gifted. However, we know that this is not true since the people that we are discussing are already in the top 10% of students in the country. They have already proven that they are gifted.

The issue here is that a student's perception of their performance is relative. It is shaped in the context of their classroom, among their peers. And one's perception of their value dramatically affects a person's willingness to tackle challenges and finish difficult tasks. Those students who believe they can do well and that they should do well have an increased willingness to tackle challenges and finish difficult tasks. Belief in self is a critical factor in motivation and confidence. Therefore, the more elite your team or the more excellent your reputation, the more you have to watch out for relative deprivation, and the more you have to guard the confidence of your people and how they see themselves regarding success. The more you have to remember that there is no spoon!

One method for increasing belief and reducing relative depravation is to make the rules work to your advantage. In *David and Goliath,* Gladwell explains that often times when we see people succeed in situations where we would have predicted failure, what we are witnessing is the result of a perceived disadvantage being exploited by someone who understands the power of playing to one's strengths. In the story that inspired the title, the central focus for almost everyone involved is how big and formidable an opponent Goliath is and how imposing of a threat he is. David, on the other hand, made the rules work to his advantage and operated in a way that set himself up for success. When David fought Goliath, he was more comfortable, fighting in a way that catered to his strengths and a way that ultimately made him superior to Goliath. And that is why David defeated Goliath.

What strengths did David have that gave him an advantage? Well, David had been successful at fighting larger, more ferocious opponents (lions and bears) before. This was an experience that not many had or would have been able, at the time, to appreciate. To David, however, this was not an outsized challenge. He had fought, and beat, wild animals who were much bigger than men and didn't fight by the rules of men. He had experienced combat where he could not get close to his foe because of the tremendous peril that it presented him. He had honed his skills as a slinger to the point where he could be confident that he could defend himself and his flock with his sling. To David, Goliath was a big, slow lion or bear that was less threatening than his previous foes because he was more predictable. David was confident in his ability to win. But only if David fought in a way that suited him.

Initially, the story tells us that David tried the traditional way. He first put on King Saul's armor and prepared for battle. He then realized that he would certainly fail if he tried it that way. He realized that he was struggling, and he also knew that he shouldn't be struggling this much if he was going to be successful. Had David continued along that path he would have surely died.

David tried to prepare to fight the traditional way, under the traditional rules, and this is what many of our people try to do. They struggle doing things in the traditional way because the systems we create do not allow for them to work to their strengths. In the end, they come up empty. And this next point is key if you are going to be the type of leader that gets your people to step into their greatness.

You must be the one to determine for them what success is, and you must do so in way that takes advantage of their strengths. Now, David was the exception to the rule. He went against the tide and determined for himself what he should do. He recognized his struggle and made the transition to a better way. However, it is important to recognize the tremendous amount of courage it takes for one to do that. David was a ten-percenter, to borrow from our analogy earlier.

For you to become the type of leader that can get the best out of anyone, you can't afford to wait for the ten-percenters to show up. You must instead make it your standard practice to make the rules work to the advantage of your team. And you know what? You're in luck! This isn't as difficult as it appears on first glance because guess who makes the rules? That's right: you!

Helping your team to master their ability to make the rules work for them is how you develop their grit and increase their willingness to tackle difficult tasks. This is how you exponentially improve their effectiveness and their morale. This is how you overcome the problem of relative deprivation by allowing your team to operate in a space where they know they can do well, that they should well, and that the rules are set up to favor their strengths.

The idea that we make our teams better by making them fight through their struggles and letting the cream rise to the top is a myth and will keep you stuck with subpar performance and high attrition rates. As Empowering Leaders, we make our teams better by recognizing when we have put them in situations where they may be uncomfortable and they may perceive that they are struggling more than they should be. First, we acknowledge their struggle and normalize it for them. Next, we earn their trust by helping them to recognize how to use their strengths to overcome obstacles. And finally, if necessary, we adjust the rules of combat to allow them to exploit their strengths. By doing this, we let them know that we believe in them, we trust them, we anticipate that they will be successful, and we are working with them to make that possible.

***

One last note about defining success. I want you to know that I understand that your team will not always be successful. I also understand that sometimes things have to get done that don't necessarily cater to your team's strengths. This should be an infrequent occurrence, however. And while it is necessary to bridge the gap and prepare your team for those rare occasions, it is the how that determines whether they will actually be able to overcome a worst-case scenario.

Sun Tzu, author of *The Art of War,* explained the how to accomplish this 2,500 years ago: "The good fighters of old first put themselves beyond the possibility of defeat, and then waited for an opportunity of defeating the enemy. To secure ourselves against defeat lies in our own hands, but the opportunity of defeating the enemy is provided by the enemy himself. Thus, the good fighter is able to secure himself against defeat but cannot make certain of defeating the enemy."

Rener Gracie, one of my Jiu Jitsu instructors and mentors, explains it like this: "When we can become comfortable in worst case scenarios, then there are no more worst-case scenarios."

The way you prepare your team for worst-case scenarios is to is to first place them beyond the possibility of defeat. Make them feel comfortable that they can handle the situation. In this way you can allow them to, as we say in the Marine Corps, thrive in chaos. The idea is that the way that you define success for your team and the way you train them must be part of a larger strategy of getting them comfortable in uncomfortable situations.

It is important to remember that this is all based on perceived reality. You must realize the impact of your mindset as the leader, versus the mindset and limited perspective of your team. You have already slain Goliath. Your perception of your team and their struggles is from the place of knowing what is necessary to accomplish the task and having already done it in most instances.

You have already become successful. That is why you are the Leader. And as the Leader, you look at certain tasks with the knowledge that they may be difficult, but they are doable. You firmly believe that you and your team can accomplish them; otherwise, you wouldn't give your team the assignment. What you have to realize however, is that, as the Teacher, part of your job is to bring your people along to the place that you are, to bridge the gap.

In order to help them understand and see the world from your perspective, you have to get them comfortable in worst case scenarios. That is not something that is learned in the fight. That is something that is trained in all of the moments where it is safe and comfortable. That feeling of safety and comfort is transferred to situations that are increasingly less safe and less comfortable. That is how you make the small gains you need to make, step by step. That is how you create sustainable growth. That is how you teach them to thrive in chaos.

Too often Leaders focus simply on the doing and not enough on the perception and the understanding of their teams. Their teams may perform well, but they don't understand how they did so. Without the understanding of the leader, they will never be able to achieve that level of success again, and they will only take from the experience the fear and the anxiety that was their reality before the success. This is the exact opposite of what we want as an Empowering Leader.

To be an Empowering Leader, you must ensure that your team not only gets the proverbial fish but that they understand how to get more fish in the future. This process of defining success, of setting them up for success, of catering to their strengths, and of bridging the gap earns you their trust so that they are excited about the projects you give. This makes them receptive to your teaching and also makes them willing to deal with temporary discomfort of the learning process.

You are changing their paradigm about success and allowing them to see the world in a different way. You are helping them to develop their own Leader's Mind.

You are slowly showing them how to bend the spoon.

You are giving them Matrix Moments.

Now, let's look at how to set up the processes and systems that reinforce the trust and belief that you are working to cultivate in your team.

SECTION 2: COMMUNICATION AND STRATEGY

Chapter 6: Many Hands Make Light Work

EM(P)OWER: Proper Delegation a.k.a. Play to Win

By defining success in a way that sets your team up for success, you are putting your team in the best possible situation for victory. This, coupled with catering to their strengths (discussed further in the next chapter), allows you to ensure that they will be able to exploit the opportunities that are provided to them. So how do we do set them up for success? Well, the first step in that process you have already done. When you ensured that your expectations were reasonable, you made sure that you were not putting undue pressure on them. You were not asking them to be perfect or beyond perfect. Thereby, you made sure that you believed that they could accomplish the task.

Step 2 is to ensure that what you ask them to do is both challenging (aspirational) and at the same time achievable without them having to give a perfect effort (inspirational). The goal is to get them to stretch outside of their comfort zones but to manage that stretch so as not to do any irreparable damage.

The best example of this balance is from the realm of physical training. So many people decide that they are going to get in shape, so they go and they do a crazy work out for about a week or two. Then, they either quit because their minds can't deal with that level of discomfort for a long period, or they injure themselves. The key to sustained, long-term growth (creating Leaders) is manageable discomfort over a consistent, prolonged period of time with adequate rest and celebration of accomplishments. By doing this, you build two things: You build your body's ability to tolerate the discomfort because your muscles adapt, and you build your mind's ability to deal with the discomfort because your mind adapts. The remaining steps in the EMPOWER Method are about creating systems and processes that allow you to manage the sustained, long-term growth of your team by putting them in situations that allow their minds and their muscles to adapt while maintaining their faith in you and, more importantly, your faith in them.

The most powerful strategy that you will use as you work to get your team to take more initiative and give their best on every project is delegation. It is important to understand that, as a Leader, your responsibility is not the work. From this point forward in your career, if you want to do bigger and better things, you can no longer focus on the work. As we discussed earlier, you must focus on the people who do the work. Mastering delegation is the principle way that Empowering Leaders play to win.

The resources related to how one properly delegates are less abundant than those resources which explain the benefits of delegation. Looking at most of what is available, it would seem that delegation is as simple as passing off your tasks to your subordinates so that you can have more time to do the important things. This misunderstanding of delegation has been a recipe for disaster. It has resulted in scores of people trying and failing to use this powerful strategy without ever truly understanding its full potential.

The idea that delegation is about passing off tasks so that you as the leader can be more effective at doing could not be further from the truth. Though efficiencies of time and effort are natural byproducts of proper delegation, approaching it this way puts the cart before the horse. In this chapter, we will focus on the purpose of delegation, the principles of delegation, and some practical application strategies. Once you understand these and have applied them to your processes, then you will be able to skillfully delegate to your teams with great success.

***

Purpose of Delegation

The purpose of Delegation is to EMPOWER. Webster's defines Delegation as: "the act of empowering to act for another." As an example of proper usage, it gives," the *delegation* of responsibilities." As you can see from the definition, the focus is on the EMPOWERing, not the act or the responsibility that you are passing off. It is about the act and the fact that you are EMPOWERing the person to do it for you. In other words, if you are not empowering, you are not delegating.

It is imperative, therefore, that we remember that what we are doing when we delegate tasks is EMPOWERing those that we lead to act for us. To do so, we must first ensure that they are capable of acting for us. If we give them the responsibility without the present capacity, we are just setting them up for failure. This is how so many leaders lose the faith of their teams. Remember: Potential is different than actual ability. And on that note, let's discuss the five key principles of proper delegation.

Principles of Proper Delegation:

These principles: Clarity, Aspiration, Inspiration, Trust, and Ownership are the foundation of effective delegation. When delegating tasks, you must make sure that your process:

1. Is Clear: You must be clear about what the tasks are and what success will look like when they are accomplished.
2. Is Aspirational: The tasks must require your team to stretch out of their comfort zone to reach them.
3. Is Inspirational: The tasks delegated, and the vision they are tied to, inspire your team to perform.
4. Generates Trust: Your team must trust that you have faith in them to handle the task they have been given.
5. Transfers Ownership: You must give the tasks to your team to take away as their own goals and objectives.

If any of these key principles are lacking in your delegation processes, then your team's performance will suffer, and you will never be able to comfortably leave them to do their jobs. You will never be able to get the time back that you need to focus on the things that are necessary to grow and improve your business or enterprise. You will be working harder and not smarter.

***

Since proper delegation is such an important part of the EMPOWER Method, let's look at these keys a little more closely.

Clarity:

Many Executing Leaders have a hard time making the transition to being Empowering Leaders because of a lack of clarity. This lack of clarity is often the result of an ineffective system for communicating that vision to the teams they lead. This is especially difficult for Executing Leaders to recognize because they have generally been thought of (by themselves and others) as good communicators. However, the communication needs of an Empowering Leader are much different than those of an Executing Leader. They have different things to accomplish and different pitfalls to look out for. (See the Obstacles chapter for an in-depth discussion of the communication process and the many causes of miscommunication.)

The objective of Empowering communication is to ensure that your team understands the goal, knows how to reach the goal, and knows how to recognize on their own if they have achieved the goal.

Aspiration

Aspiration is the hope of achieving something. It is different from the stimulation to do something which is inspiration. Aspiration is the stretching, the hoping, the believing that something is possible. Aspiration can also serve as inspiration, however. It is Aspiration that comes first if great things are to get accomplished. For the purpose of the Empowering Leader, your job is to constantly cultivate your team's Aspirations. Cultivating Aspiration is nurturing the hope, the belief of your team in themselves that they can accomplish what they have not accomplished before. It is the continual renewing of their faith in themselves while at the same time challenging them to dream bigger and believe more. Aspiration is the foundation of delegation; it is the belief that EMPOWERs them to do.

Inspiration and Trust

Inspiration and Trust are the kindred spirits of this process. Trust is the underpinning of everything that we will do as leaders. Your job is to create a space where your team feels safe, where they feel like you believe in them, where they can make mistakes and not feel like they will be judged by what happens on their worst day. As you inspire your team to reach for the greatness, as you remind them why you selected them (or why they were selected, if you didn't) for this team, as you focus their minds on their strengths and capabilities, you will build their trust in you. These are things that you are constantly working on throughout the EMPOWER Method process and throughout your leadership journey.

Remember that our goal as Empowering Leaders, is to work ourselves out of a job. In order to do that, you must be able to facilitate your team's transition from dependence to independence to interdependence. You must constantly inspire them to keep going and to trust themselves to perform. The more they trust that you believe in them, the more they are motivated to do the work, the better results they will have and the more they will believe in themselves and in the process.

Ownership:

In keeping with the idea of helping them transition from dependence to independence, the concept of ownership is key. Your team must learn to take ownership of their actions, their roles, their responsibilities, and most importantly, their results. The problem that arises here is that most Managers teach ownership by accountability and lecturing about responsibility. This is the wrong way to accomplish the objective.

By holding people accountable in the traditional sense and droning on about personal responsibility, Managers separate themselves from those they lead and take on the air of a puritanical preacher. I have often struggled with this in my life as a parent. I sometimes chuckle at the irony. I have mastered these principles, been tremendously successful, and even won awards when leading people to accomplish objectives in my professional life, yet when I am trying to get my children to go to bed, do their chores, practice for sports, or be more respectful, you would sometimes think I have no idea what I am doing.

These principles are the same, however. In order to get people to take ownership, you have to create an environment where there are no other options than to take ownership. See, one of the biggest problems with not allowing our team to make mistakes is that we take away their ownership of those mistakes. We feel like we are responsible for the mistakes that they make. This leads us to become controlling leaders rather than Empowering Leaders. And the more we try to control, the less they take ownership.

If your goal is to EMPOWER, you will have less control inherently. If you can give away that control, then your people can truly take ownership. We will discuss how to do so in the Establish Roles section below, but suffice it to say, transferring ownership of the consequences and the responsibility for dealing with those consequences is a major part of delegation.

Applying the 5 Keys-Establishing Roles

So now you should understand the principles of delegation (Clarity, Aspiration, Inspiration, Trust, and Ownership). Do you remember how we discussed in the Evaluate Your Expectations chapter the need for you to be clear on what you are trying to do and whether your team can do it? You will be using these SMART goals structure to evaluate your goals at every level of the EMPOWER process. So, after you have finished this chapter, feel free to go back and look at the previous two chapters through the SMART lens.

As we discussed in the previous chapter, setting SMART goals is the method we use to achieve our leadership communication objectives and to delegate appropriately. SMART goals allow our teams to be clear on what it is they are to accomplish and will also allow both them and us to know when they have done so. Embedded within this method are mechanisms for tackling Aspiration, Inspiration, Trust, and Ownership. To recap SMART is an acronym that stands for:

S - Specific

M - Measurable

A - Achievable/Assignable

R - Relevant

T - Time Bound

So how do we set SMART goals? To give us a break from looking at this from the leader's perspective, let's look at the how to do this from a vantage point that everyone is familiar with: New Year's Resolutions.

Each year, millions of people make a new year's resolution. Many, however, really have no idea of what they are really trying to do (no clarity). They set themselves up for failure because they have no method for measuring whether they have been successful or not. For example, people say, "I'm going to work out more this year." Sounds reasonable, right?

At first glance, it doesn't sound that bad, but then when you start trying to define what that looks like, you begin to see how this goal-setting experience is more likely than not going to end in disaster and disappointment. In leadership terms we might say things like, "We want to increase productivity this year." Let's look at why this doesn't work.

It is likely that the person who says that they want to "work out more this year" has some body appearance or health issues that they want to address. They also know that working out more is better for them than working out less. So, in their mind, working out more is the cure for these other issues. However, that is generally the extent of their analysis. This is how their resolution plays out.

They begin working out two or three times a week. This works for the first week. By the second week their workout regimen has begun to conflict with their schedule. They also have to deal with being very sore and the realization that they are in worse shape than they originally thought. Herein begins the cycle of negative thoughts. Each workout is harder and harder to be excited about, and therefore, they start missing.

By the end of the month, they are only working out maybe one or two more times than before the New Year or possibly only as much as they used to work out before. They are also beginning to get bored with the workouts they are doing. They start to encounter, all over again, the obstacles that they often faced last year which made them not work out as much as they would have liked. Additionally, they haven't seen the results that they envisioned when they made the resolution, even though they feel they have been working hard, so they begin to work out even less.

At this point, they work out maybe once or twice every other week for the next month and by the beginning of month 3 they quit working out altogether. They feel like a failure every time they think back to this, and therefore, when they think about starting back up, they get discouraged because they feel it will be just like this. The fact is that that they actually met their goal which was to work out more this year. The problem was not the effort; the problem was the goal setting process. Now let's revise this goal using SMART goal setting.

Specific

The first thing that would need to be done would be to set a more specific goal. The original was "to work out more this year." This needs more definition as it is very ambiguous in its current state. It is easy to get in the weeds with our definitions. Our goal is to be specific enough that we can be certain that anyone walking in off the street could understand what we are trying to do. We want to eliminate as many specialized words as possible. Once we can do that, then we can know that the people whom we are delegating tasks to will know what they are supposed to be doing.

To do so in this case, we can get more clarity by defining what a workout is, how long a workout is, how many calories we burn during a workout, etc. In this current example, our goal has no clarity because the words we use to define it don't give us any. Both "workout" and "more" are ambiguous. Therefore, we need to resolve this ambiguity.

For the sake of this example, workout will be simply defined as any physical exercise routine lasting longer than twenty minutes.

Note: It is a necessary ground rule of the goal-setting process that a goal has to have terms that are easily defined and unambiguous. Clarity is key!

Measurable

The next step is to make your goal is measurable. We need one of two measurements since our goal is to work out more. We must either know how much we worked out last year, or we need to change our goal a bit so that it reflects how much we actually want to work out this year. Either way, we will have a measurement that is not as vague as more. For this example, let's say that we want to work out at least two times per week.

Note: This is one of the most critical steps of this process. Embedded in this step are the principles of Clarity (You have to know what it is to measure it), Ownership (You are not the only one that measures it. Everyone can), and Trust (Your team can have certainty regarding when they have done a good job). The more you develop good measuring processes, the higher your team morale will be and the more work you will be able to delegate.

Attainable/Assignable

A crucial component of goal setting is whether the goal is attainable. This inquiry is important because we must be realistic about what we are trying to do. Sometimes we set ourselves up for failure by not taking into account the difficulty others will encounter to complete a task and subsequently not formulating a plan to overcome that difficulty.

Though nothing is impossible, there are many things that are extremely difficult. It is important that we treat these difficult tasks with the proper amount of respect for how hard they will be to accomplish. If we don't, then we won't prepare ourselves mentally for the challenge, and we also won't give ourselves, or our teams, the tools which are necessary to accomplish the objective.

For this example, we must look at potential barriers to accomplishment (Threat/Risk Analysis) like how much time do we have available to workout per week. We must also look at whether we are going to go to a gym or workout at home. Do we have the facilities/programs at home, or will we need to go to a gym? If we need to go to a gym, do we have the money to pay for one? Do we have a gym membership already? Do we want to go to a gym, or will that be a barrier to us accomplishing the goal? If it is a barrier, can we easily overcome that barrier? If we can't easily overcome it, does it make us want to change the goal?

As you can see, this inquiry must be extensive. It is also ongoing. This is the most left out portion of the process, and that is why so many objectives fail before they begin. It is also tragic because completing this part well can do so much to inform the other areas of our process.

For purposes of our example, let's make it easy and say that we can work out at home, and we already have a program that we like and have the time to complete the workouts. Therefore, this goal ranks high on our achievability scale. The scale goes from 1 (very low attainability/hard to achieve) to 10 (very high attainability/easy to achieve). Our goal would get somewhere between a 7 and 10.

Note: This step has Aspiration and Inspiration imbedded all throughout it. One of the reasons that you want to have a high score is because your belief in your team's success is greater the easier the task. They will be able to feel this, and it will inspire your team to accomplish the task. Similarly, when you have a score that is in the 7-8 range, you still have that belief that they will be able to accomplish it, but they also know that it will stretch them a bit.

Whenever you are delegating, you should strive to ensure that the tasks you delegate have a high achievability score. While it is acceptable to delegate lower scored tasks, if the you are not aware of the obstacles they present, you are simply setting your people up for failure. Remember that the purpose of delegating is to EMPOWER your team to act for you. If you have not set up the tasks to have high achievability scores, you are not empowering unless you create an extra safe space for them to make mistakes and learn (more on this point in the next chapter). Always know that if a task is difficult for you, your expectations for your team should be that it will be difficult. They can always surprise you, but, again, you always want to have reasonable expectations.

Relevant

Next, we must ensure that our goal is relevant. This is where we look at the "why" of our goal. Why are we trying to work out more? What is working out more going to accomplish for us? How is achieving this goal linked to our larger mission and to our vision? This lets us know which type of workouts we can choose and will also help us in the future to determine whether the course of action we took was the most effective one.

For this example, the relevance of working out is that we want to be healthier, to feel stronger, and to look more toned and cut in our muscles. Again, it is possible to go into more detail about what that actually means because those could be vague notions as well. However, for the sake of brevity we are not going to do that here. Just note that by referencing our "why," we attach our goal to another goal which we should be ensuring also follows the SMART strategy. Our goals are then more likely to be accomplished because they are linked to other objectives that we have in our lives.

Note: Showing your team the relevance of your goals to theirs is the key to building up their trust of you. Your team must understand your why even more than they understand your what. They must know why you set the goals that you do. They need to be able to get behind the mission of what you are doing. Your objective when setting goals should be to always make them congruent with the why that made your team members want to be on the team in the first place. By doing so, you allow them to see that giving their all on the projects that you present to them actually moves them closer toward their goals.

It is also imperative that you keep fidelity with the purpose and values of your team. This will generate a level of trust in you from your team members that will allow you to make mistakes and them to still follow you and believe in you. It will also make them willing to work harder for you than they would even be willing to work for themselves. As we have discussed, trust is everything.

Time Bound

Lastly, the goal must be time-bound. This is an important factor because this lets us know when we can and should evaluate the goal. Again, your time limits will largely affect your measurement of your goal. In our current example, we want to work out two to three times per week but we haven't decided for how long. Do we want to do this for one month, two months, six months, the year, forever? If we go back to our original premise of more than last year, we could simply approximate how much we worked out last year and break down how much we would have to work out each week to match that number. For the sake of this example, we are going to say that we have a three-month goal.

Note: When Delegating, this practice is important for two reasons.

1) It adds clarity to your goal. By giving a time limit to the goal, we immediately know how long the effort to accomplish it is necessary. We are also better equipped to prioritize the work necessary to accomplish the goal.

2) It allows your team to take ownership of the goal, and it allows you to release it to them. Having an agreed upon timeline creates an objective measurement of performance. Rather than having to check up on your people, you can have them evaluate their performance rather than having to come to you to do so. This also allows you to break the tasks up into smaller pieces if necessary. All in all, you are able to get more of the tasks off of your plate once you can determine a timeline for their accomplishment.

So now, let's look at our original goal in comparison with our SMART goal:

Regular Goal	Smart Goal
To work out more this year than last year.	We are going to work out two to three times per week for three months. Our desired result is to feel stronger and look more toned and cut in our muscles at the end of that three months. This is connected to our larger goal of living a healthy lifestyle. This is a highly attainable goal because we already have a program that we like at home and the space and time necessary to accomplish the goal. We will track the goal by using a wall calendar to mark off the days that we work out. We will measure our progress weekly.

As you can see, the SMART goal is much clearer. It allows anyone looking at it to get a clear picture of what is supposed to be accomplished. It also makes measurement a critical component of the goal itself, not some afterthought. Additionally, the SMART goal allows space for us to Evaluate our Expectations as we create the goal and to manage for risks that we may not have been thinking about.

Lastly, the goal is attached to a larger goal that reminds anyone who is reading it why it is being attempted. The great thing about the SMART goals process is that by going through it you make achieving your objectives more likely. An added bonus, which we will discuss more in the Engage Their Inner Problem-Solver Chapter, is that even when these types of goals are not achieved, we have a wealth of information to inform us how to improve the next time we attempt to accomplish this objective or any other related project.

***

One thing that I want to say to you before you begin to attempt to implement this strategy is this: It's okay if you are not a rockstar at the beginning. This is a delegation process, not a delegation activity. You are going to be constantly tweaking this process as you gain a better understanding of the key principles and are better able to apply the SMART goal setting process to all areas of your enterprise.

With that understood, it is important that when you establish roles and give out tasks that you consider the principles we have discussed thus far which will set your team up for success. Don't focus on making your team members work in their weaknesses; instead, set them up for what they are best at doing.

In the 1990s, and especially from 1996-1998, the Chicago Bulls were one of the greatest basketball teams in the NBA, possibly of all time. During that time they had Michael Jordan, Scottie Pippen, Ron Harper, Steve Kerr, Dennis Rodman, and Luc Longley. Each of the players on that team had a particular set of skills. Now, Michael Jordan was undeniably the best player in basketball at the time and, in my humble opinion, at any time. However, basketball is a team sport. Therefore, no matter how great Michael was, he could not score all the points, defend all the players on the other team, and get all the rebounds. So what did the Bulls do to make their team so successful?

Let's look at the rest of the players and how the coach of the Bulls, Phil Jackson, put them in the best positions he could to get the team a victory. Dennis Rodman was not the best shooter; as a matter of fact, he was possibly one of the worst on the team. Steve Kerr was not a large guard and not a particularly great defender. Luc Longley was not tremendously big or athletic for a center, and Scottie Pippen and Ron Harper, while pretty good all-around players, were not outstanding in any one area of their games. So, was Phil Jackson's coaching strategy to set up practices, set plays, and schemes to try to make these players improve in their weaker areas? No!

He focused on their strengths. Dennis Rodman was one of the best rebounders in the history of the NBA and a phenomenal defender. Steve Kerr is one of the best three-point shooters in NBA History. Luc Longley, Scottie Pippen, and Ron Harper were great role players and had developed phenomenal work ethic. Using these strengths, Phil Jackson set up his system to maximize the strengths of this team's members and to optimize the way that their strengths played off of each other. Teams had the hardest time accounting for everything the Bulls could throw at them because if you took away one of their strengths they used another. This formula helped them to win three straight championships and to set a league Win/Loss record of 72-10 that stood for nearly twenty years.

In summary, as you delegate tasks to your team, always remember that you are to focus first on your ability to empower them to accomplish these tasks. Once you have done that, you want to empower your team as a whole by ensuring that you establish roles and hand out tasks in a way that capitalizes on the talents of your team rather than trying to get them to fit some preconceived notion of how you think the roles should be. You want to deal with the team that you have and maximize their strengths. That is how you can make the amazing happen.

Chapter 7: Resilience Is the Foundation of Success

"There are no secrets to success. It is the result of preparation, hard work and learning from failure." - Colin Powell

"Every adversity, every failure, every heartache carries with it the seed of a greater or equal benefit." - Napoleon Hill

"Don't be afraid to fail. Don't waste energy trying to cover up failure. Learn from your failures and go on to the next challenge. It's ok to fail. If you're not failing, you're not growing." - H. Stanley Judd

EMP(O)WER: Optimize Your Environment for Growth

In order to help your team be their best, to cultivate leaders, to truly empower them, you have to fundamentally change the way they view failure. You have to get them to embrace the idea that it is okay to fail early, fail often, and fail forward.

When we are trying to be more successful, changing your own paradigm around failure and that of your team is the key to the biggest breakthroughs.

Failing Is Bad... Or is it?

In almost every aspect of our childhood years we are taught that failure is bad. Most parents discipline their children for bad behavior much more often than they praise them for good behavior. We are told no as children much more often than we are told yes. The focus of most parenting is preventing wrong, rather than promoting right. See Chapter 10 for more discussion on the important distinction between positive reinforcement versus negative reinforcement.

This is continued in our education system. In our schools, teachers grade papers by letting you know how many questions you got wrong. Our grading scales are set up so that only those who are correct 70% of the time or more are able to pass a class. We expel children for behavior that we feel is counterproductive, and we have rules in place now that suspend kids from school for fighting, even if they were only defending themselves. We have begun to punish children for making the mistake of not avoiding someone else's failure.

This training and attitude continue into our institutions of higher education. In college, you study for classes and are given three or four major opportunities to show that you know the information (mid-terms, finals, and a couple of quizzes or papers depending on the discipline). Those who make the fewest mistakes earn the prizes of high GPAs and top honors at graduation.

The conventional idea is that you put pressure on people and the cream will rise to the top. But this idea approaches performance from the wrong angle. This is a formula for weeding out, for determining who are the best in a group given very narrow parameters around what is considered best. We rarely stop to ask ourselves whether or not this is actually preparing us (or those we lead) for success. The weeding out method may work as a screening tool, but it is an abysmal failure when the goal is growth and development.

Generally, putting the pressure of mistake-proof living into your system constraints actually makes people perform worse, not better. (See the discussion on "Relative Deprivation" in the last chapter.) It causes us to relate struggling to inadequacy. Left unchecked, it causes people to abandon their dreams and never truly reach their full potential. This is because they get trapped into the belief that because they have struggled and at times failed, they were not good enough. This is the paradigm our educational system prepares us to believe. However, this is the exact opposite of the thought process that is needed for success.

These are the people that make up the teams that we lead. People who are products of that system. People who believe that failure is bad. People who focus more on the consequences of mistakes and less on the spoils of victory. People who know that if they mess up they could lose everything and therefore decide to play it safe. And guess what? You play into that belief every time you save them from failure.

***

Here's the secret of this book that I hope you have been coming to realize. You are a major part of why your people can just do their jobs!

Unknowingly, every day, you reinforce the paradigm that they have learned their entire lives. You are successful because you don't make mistakes. You are in charge because you do it right. You correct them when they do it wrong, and you are the one that tells them how to do it better. You have all the answers. When they have a problem, you fix it because it is easier to tell them how to fix it than it is to show them.

When they look at how your processes and systems work, what they see is this: Those that don't make mistakes are the ones that succeed. Therefore, since they are smart, smarter than we often times give them credit for, they limit their mistakes. They make sure that they don't do anything without your permission or prior approval. It's OK that getting this project done may take a week longer doing it your way. That's not their problem since that week is because it takes you that long to approve it. They pass the responsibility for all decision making to the person who has already demonstrated they can handle it, YOU.

This is why you can't delegate anything properly, and this is why it feels like they are not doing their jobs. They are simply doing what they have been trained to do. They are minimizing mistakes. They are coloring within the lines. They are making sure that they don't do anything that might get them fired. They are playing not to lose rather than playing to win.

So how do you change that? How do you get them break out of that limiting system? You develop systems that encourage them to fail early, to fail often, and to fail forward.

***

Done Is Better Than Perfect

As I have told you, I am a recovering perfectionist and there was a point that this paradigm was taking a tremendous toll on my family. Because of my need to cross every T and dot every I, I spent way too much time at work. Everything had to be perfect because, in my mind, if anything was messed up, that is all people would remember. And I represented more than just me. My work was how people would judge my worth and the worth of others who looked like me or had the same last name I did. If I made mistakes, I would then have to spend time I didn't have trying to win back their trust of my capabilities. I don't know if you have ever felt that type of pressure, but for me it was becoming unbearable.

Then, one of my mentors in Real Estate Development, Than Merrill, said something at a conference I attended that truly changed my life. It was during a course where he was talking about getting things done and analysis paralysis. He helped us to see how many of our best ideas never see the light of day because of our fear of making mistakes. He explained how this had happened to him as well. And then he gave us this mantra, which he used to overcome this problem. It went like this:

"Done is better than perfect."

Here was a man who had graduated from Yale University, played professional football, and built a real estate development company that was one of the most profitable and fastest growing in the country, and he was telling me that he struggled like I did and, more importantly, that it was okay to not be perfect. It was like a weight was lifted off of my shoulders. Although looking back, I can see that the universe had been telling me this for many years, it wasn't until this moment that I could see the blessing of mistakes.

During that seminar, Than continued to explain how much we learn from the first version of anything and how awesome it is in the production and planning process to have a prototype to work with. After the seminar, I began to re-read many of the books that I had read on leadership and success with new eyes. All of the quotes about failure and how important it is to success seemed like they were highlighted now. I wondered how could I have missed them before. That moment is when my paradigm shifted, and I hope that you get to experience that shift.

Failing is good. It may not be what you want, but it will definitely be what you need. Failing is going to happen if you are trying to do anything great. If you are trying to grow, if you are trying to empower anyone else, you will fail along the way. The question is not: "Will you fail?" But rather: "How will you react when it happens?"

It is my belief that you will serve your team best if you set up plenty of opportunities for them to fail and to learn that failure is part of the process of success. Failing and getting up from that failure builds resiliency... and resiliency is the foundation for success. Therefore, this chapter is dedicated to how you create your systems and manage your deadlines in such a way that you allow your team to feel comfortable failing, getting up and brushing off, and getting back in the ring. My favorite quote that kind of summarizes the feeling that you want to cultivate on your team comes from Teddy Roosevelt and it goes like this:

"It is not the critic who counts; not the man who points out how the strong man stumbles, or where the doer of deeds could have done them better. The credit belongs to the man who is actually in the arena, whose face is marred by dust and sweat and blood; who strives valiantly; who errs, who comes short again and again, because there is no effort without error and shortcoming; but who does actually strive to do the deeds; who knows great enthusiasms, the great devotions; who spends himself in a worthy cause; who at the best knows in the end the triumph of high achievement, and who at the worst, if he fails, at least fails while daring greatly, so that his place shall never be with those cold and timid souls who neither know victory nor defeat."

Make this quote part of your introduction to every new member of your team. Make this your team motto. Incorporate it however you can because you want your team to be in the arena. You want to develop a culture where it is more important to produce something. You want your people to understand that they can only learn from the doing, and therefore, as long as what they are doing is with pure intention and it's living up to the reasonable expectations that you have set, what they are doing will be celebrated.

But wait... Won't that just make more work to clean up later? Won't productivity suffer? Won't they just get comfortable with their mistakes? The answer is NO! And here is why...

You always Fail Forward!

***

Failing Forward

By creating an environment where mistakes are not heretical, we create an environment where learning from mistakes can happen. Not only can it happen, but it is expected and celebrated. It's been said before, "If you're not failing, you're not trying!" and I completely agree. In an environment where learning from mistakes is possible, and more importantly, celebrated, growth is inevitable. And this is not just your basic arithmetic progression. I am talking about spurting, bursting, exponential growth.

The reason for this is that you begin to operate in the synergies of community learning, i.e., interdependence. In this type of environment, 1+1 does not equal 2. It equals 11 or 1100 or 11 million. As Steven Covey explained in *The 7 Habits of Highly Effective People,* synergy can happen in this environment because everyone is learning from everyone else, and that includes you. Later in the book we will get into the specifics of how the learning that spurs this growth happens. However, in this chapter we are going to discuss how to set up your systems and processes so that the environment is prepared for the type of engagement we will discuss later.

So... How do we encourage the "Done is Better than Perfect!" mindset while maintaining our production quality and our deadlines?

We manage our deadlines to promote our people to fail earlier, more often, and in more manageable ways.

***

As leaders we often look at a project and create deadlines based on one of two methods. The method we select mostly depends on how much we trust our team. If there is a high level of trust (indicated by the fact that we know if it is wrong they will work with us after hours if necessary to fix it), then we will allow them to let us know how much time they think the task will take, and then we will build in a buffer. If there is a low level of trust (read: people we feel we need to micromanage), then we reverse-engineer our timelines to be based on how long we think it will take us to either do the job ourselves or hold their hand while they do the job. We then make our preliminary deadlines based on how much buffer we believe that we need.

Both of these methods create a buffer that takes responsibility for meeting the final deadline back from our subordinates and places it squarely on our shoulders. These methods do not really transfer the ownership of the task. It's more like we use them to allow our team to borrow the task for a while. The problem is this: Everyone knows that it is fake. You know it, your team knows it, and they know that you know it. Therefore, this scenario works to severely erode your trust in them and their trust in you.

So, how do we do it differently?

You must manage your deadlines in a completely different way. You set your deadlines up as opportunities for your team to fail and still be okay because they still have time to get feedback, rethink their approach, and to fix the problem. Your role in a truly delegated situation is empowerment and facilitation, not management. I realized the power of this principle in my own life as I made the transition from college to graduate school.

In college, I was phenomenal at all-night paper writing (not really but just stick with me here). You see, I was one of those people that did my best work under the stress of the deadline. At least that is what I told myself. I thought I was really good at writing a paper the night before it was due, turning it in, and getting a decent grade. This was actually a true assessment if I only included the papers that I turned in on time in that calculation.

But that's the problem; those weren't the only papers I wrote or didn't write. If I had taken all the papers that I wrote or was supposed to write while I was in college and evaluated this method fairly, I would have seen that this was not a very successful method of accomplishing my best work. Upon graduation, and looking at that permanent 2.4 G.P.A, I had to begin eating that humble pie I had been avoiding the past five years. As I began graduate school, I decided to look at things differently and try things differently.

I began to write my papers three days before they were due. I would then leave them for a day and revisit them the day before they were due, make whatever edits I thought were needed, and turn them in one day early. I was amazed at the quality of my work following this process. I was also amazed at how work that I thought was my best, and admittedly was pretty good, was so much less than what I was capable of.

What I learned from this was two-fold:
1. I was capable of way more than I thought
2. We reinforce our limits by the stories that we tell ourselves.

When I was in undergrad, I would often not write a paper because I didn't feel like it. I didn't feel like I could do my best work, and since I knew that my best work was necessary for me to finish in the timeframe that I left for myself, I would just not do the work. I would rather not try than fail. I once got a B+ in a class in which I didn't turn in a paper that was worth nearly 10% of my grade. It still makes me sick to think that if I would have just turned in a paper, even if I only got a 50% on it, I would have gotten an A in the class. But this was the loop I was stuck in.

And this is the loop that many of your people are stuck in based on the deadlines that you give them. You put things out so that they are off of your plate, and you trust them to do what they are supposed to do. You then come in and check on them in time to make sure that they are far enough along that it won't be a complete disaster. Every once in a while, there is a major problem, but your most common problem is that they seem to be doing fine until it's time to turn in the final project.

Then you realize that the work that they put together is C work at best. This is frustrating because you gave them all the tools they needed, you told them to come to you if they had any problems, you gave them clear instructions, and you know they are capable of more. You are frustrated and they are frustrated.

You feel like you have done all you can to help them, and they feel like they did what you asked, so why is there a problem? Aside from the issues that we have already discussed in previous chapters with communication of our goals, there is another problem showing up here which is very common. This problem comes from the inability to distinguish between management as supervision versus facilitation as supervision. While many people think that these are the same, that is not true. It is especially not true in the context of Leadership.

Supervise

In the Marine Corps, there is an acronym for everything, and the Marine Leader's planning process is no different. BAMCIS is the acronym used to explain the steps for leading Marines. It stands for:

B - Begin Planning

A - Arrange Reconnaissance

M - Make Reconnaissance

C - Complete the Plan

I - Implement the Plan

S - Supervise

While most people excel at the first five steps, the last one is what trips people up. The same is in the civilian world. This is because the first five rely on the leader to perform. The leader can do them at times that are convenient and can make them as perfect as they want. Problem is, the money is made in the sixth step. This is where the proverbial rubber meets the road. And this is where most plans and most planners fall down.

And this takes us back to that quote from my mentor, "Done is better than perfect!" The reason that this works is because, without your people doing something, there is really nothing to improve, nothing to make perfect, nothing to supervise. A plan is just that, an idea. It is not a real thing; it is full of potential energy, none of it realized. And this is what your plan, your project, or your process is until your people start doing it: potential.

You have no idea if you were really clear in your instructions or your expectations until they start working on it. And this is the reason that you want to get them working and getting you feedback as quickly as possible. This is also why you must create a safe space for them to give you this feedback and to make mistakes. You only become a better leader in an environment where you can gain authentic critique of your leadership. That only happens when it is safe for your people to make mistakes, an environment where you are a facilitator rather than a manager.

***

So, what does that look like in reality? It looks like more deadlines and not less. You do this by instituting frequent quality controls into your processes. For example, take our story about Andrew and Jeremy from the introduction. If you had an employee like Jeremy, at the end of your exchange, it would be reasonable to feel like he underperformed again, even though you gave him all the freedom he should have needed to demonstrate his talent. When he and you are at work again together on Monday, you would call him in and let him know how you would have liked the project to be done, and you would tell him to feel free to come to you with questions earlier if there is something that he doesn't understand in the future. The whole talk would take you about thirty minutes because you are inserting so much of puff into the conversation. You don't want to shut him down and make him feel like you don't believe in him. Or conversely, you give it to him straight, but there is constant back and forth with him deflecting blame and trying to save face. Either way, thirty minutes are gone.

What happens next?

He leaves your office feeling like he did what you asked and that you are just too hard to please. "If you want the stuff done a certain way, then just tell me exactly what you want and I can make it," he thinks. He also notices that you didn't say anything about the graphics that he put in which, by the way, you didn't include in your original request. You did notice them, and they were tremendously helpful to your presentation. You meant to talk about them; however, you forgot while you were trying to get him to understand how he could have done the task better if he would have just followed your instructions.

Jeremy is now more dedicated to doing exactly what you say and not wasting any time doing anything extra. His performance improves regarding the things you went over with him, but the next time he leaves something else out that you didn't say explicitly. Of course, you feel like you shouldn't have had to say it. He also has begun to bring everything to you and ask you questions about everything. This makes his performance better, but it is taking more and more of your time to manage him. It seems like in order to improve his performance, you have had to work harder. That is the opposite of what we want, but it is routine when we practice the lending method of delegation.

***

Using frequent check-ins, which I call Quality Control (QC) checks, this scenario plays out a bit differently. Before you even give the task to your team, you will have already done the SMART goal-setting process. Therefore, you know how you are going to measure completion (Measurement is Critical). You then break up that measurement process into steps where you can gauge their progress and thereby gauge the likelihood of completion of the goal earlier in the process. Remember our idea of a calendar where we were able to check off workout days.

Once you have these intervals decided, you think about the questions that you can ask during those intervals to check the progress. The questions are one of the key differences here. Instead of looking for fires to put out, you are looking for signals that proper progress is occurring. You have to develop the questions you can ask to guide your team in the right direction regarding the things they should take as next steps. This helps you to be relieved from actually having to do the work, and it makes the situation safe for them to create the solution.

Though this may seem like it will create more work, it actually creates less. It does so because, as you are working through your quality control checks, you actually challenge your people to be their best. You also show them that, though you may know how to do something, you trust that they will be able to get the job done. By your questioning, you also signal that you are paying attention to what they are doing. In this way, you are facilitating their growth in multiple ways. They are the actors, they do the work, and your trust and belief in them is evident in all that you do.

Our example from earlier looks like this in the EMPOWER method. You give your team member the task to create the PowerPoint presentation; however, instead of giving him the deadline of one week before the presentation, you set up your quality control checks once per week for ten minutes apiece. These are checks that he knows are coming and are a part of the routine for the project from the first meeting. In QC check one, you just look at the framework that he has put together for the presentation, and you let him know some of the things that you are planning on doing with the presentation. You ask him if are there any elements of the presentation that are unclear from your instructions. He says no, and the meeting ends. You only spend about five minutes in this meeting.

QC check two is one week later. He is excited to show you some of the graphics that he has created to put into the presentation. You let him know that you think they are awesome, and you ask him if he has had any problems including the additional information that you requested. He lets you know that he wasn't aware of the additional information. You recap the highlights from the email, and you both brainstorm ideas about how to incorporate the information into the presentation. You forward him the email directly after your brainstorming session. Ten minutes here.

QC Check 2.5 is a quick five minute follow up a couple of days later, where he comes to you with a problem regarding some of the information you requested. You help him think of solutions to the problem and how he is going to solve it. You agree to his suggestion. He thanks you for your time, and he goes back to work on the project.

QC check three is the final reveal where you sit down with him and review the measurement criteria that you gave him at the beginning of the project. While you are both going through everything, he realizes that he missed one critical element, before you point it out or even notice it. You discuss how that happened, and he suggests things that he can do to make sure he doesn't forget it the next time. His suggestion is so insightful that it becomes something that you decide to implement for all of your staff while delegating tasks going forward. He lets you know that he is going to work on that tonight and have it to you tomorrow. He gets it back to you the next day, and you are thrilled with the presentation. Ten minutes here.

You go and present the next week, and when he gets back from his day off, you discuss with him and everyone else in your staff meeting how awesome the presentation was and how great a job he did making it happen. You are happy and feel like he is really starting to get this. You feel like next time you might only need two QC checks instead of three because of how he saw the problem and how he thought about fixing it. He feels empowered, trusted, and like he is really getting to understand how you think and what you need. He is excited to work on the next project that you give him and even more excited to try to impress you with his graphic artist capabilities.

Minimizing Fear of Failure & Maximizing the Second Try

This result was possible because of the fact that you minimized his fear of failure, and you maximized his second try. In the QC checks that you had with your team member, you were not telling him how he was doing things wrong. There was no need to. He had three weeks to do a project that took one week, so there was plenty of time for him to figure it out on his own. All he needed from you was the encouragement that he was doing it right and some gentle nudges in the right direction if he was messing up, which he was. The most important piece to that puzzle is that he felt like it was okay when he messed up and like he wasn't losing face by bringing those things to you. He even called your attention to something that he had missed and took initiative to fix it, without prompting. Similarly, you were at no point of time having anxiety about the project because you frequently got to see how he was working on it and how he was progressing.

You are only able to lead this way when you trust the process. You are only able to trust the process when you set the process up to succeed in spite of failure. Many times we set up our deadlines for best case scenarios. That is what I used to do when I wrote papers in college. If everything worked out and I got inspired at the right time, then I could write an amazing paper. But what if everything didn't work out.? What was the plan then? There was none.

Instead of planning for everything to work out perfectly, what Empowering Leaders do is plan for the failures and the unexpected things to happen and then use those failures as building blocks for future successes. By allowing the time for your team to ask questions and make mistakes early on, you improve their chances dramatically of getting to the right answer. Remember, part of figuring out what works is figuring out what doesn't.

Similarly, by asking was there anything that he didn't understand, after he had begun working on the project, you gave him the chance to give you feedback on your delivery at a time when that feedback is actually meaningful. When I was in the Marine Corps, the expression "drinking from a firehose" was often used to describe the classes that we received. Instructors would cover mountains of information in a two-hour session which we were to later use and be tested on. Inevitably, when they would ask for questions at the end of the session, there would be very few hands that went up. This was not an indication that we didn't have questions, it was an indication that we could not at the moment even formulate the many questions in our head into anything that would help to clarify the fog of information in our heads. If the professor took our silence as an endorsement of their teaching, they were sadly mistaken.

The same is true for leaders. Often times, right when you give an assignment, your people have no idea of the struggles they are going to have. If you institute QC checks, you provide them the opportunities when they are not taking you away from something more important to clear things up for them. This returns major dividends to your leading and teaching methods and to their confidence and their end product.

Lastly, I want to talk about Maximizing the Second Try and the issues of time and energy efficiency. Optimizing your opportunities for growth allows for your people to get two bites at the apple every time. It's like what I did when I would take a day and then review my papers. Inevitably, I would find grammar errors, spelling errors, and transition or logic errors that I had missed completely the first time through. This allowed me to make my papers so much better.

Similarly for your team, having the pattern of turning in work in enough time to review it before it is truly due allows them and you to catch things that get missed in the hustle and the bustle of normal deadlines. Enlisting them in that process makes them the quality control people and not you. It makes them responsible for the output, not you. It allows them to have the same answers that you do. Ultimately, it empowers them to take ownership of the task instead of just lending them the work.

Remember, "done is better than perfect" because done allows us to critique an actual thing and to really work towards perfection. Only when you get your people to produce and produce early, expecting to improve later, can you get to the best work that they can produce. Only when they are comfortable enough to make mistakes and ask questions and try new things will you be able to maximize the strengths that they have, many of them being strengths in areas where even you are weak. Then your team can be like the Bulls of the '90s and be much more than just the sum of its parts.

***

Does following the Leader's Way take longer and require more energy? Yes and No...

If you look at both scenarios, you will see that you spent about thirty minutes with your employee reviewing the project in each. The difference was in the result and in how that thirty minutes was broken up. In the first scenario, the thirty minutes was not scheduled. That was thirty minutes that had to come from somewhere else, and it was thirty minutes that left both parties feeling worse off.

This EMPOWER method works because it saves you many of these impromptu meetings that are really time and energy drainers. No one really likes them, and they don't really accomplish much. However, because the relationship and trust between the parties hasn't been built up, because the environment hasn't been prepared for you to check in on your people without them feeling like they are doing something wrong, we resort to the impromptu method in order to satisfy our doubts and fears about the project being done on time or correctly.

But there is another way, and this way works. The EMPOWER method removes the fear of failure and shows those that we lead how to use their failures as foundation for success. It helps them to develop the resilience necessary to be successful. It shows them how to embrace failure and to be proactive when we realize something isn't working. It also reinforces the truth that we trust them, we believe that they are capable, and that we trust in the system we have created for them to follow.

By leading in this manner, you facilitate their growth. You make them confident in their abilities and more likely to stretch to grow. You help them to aspire to greatness. This is one of the key components of this program that helps you to develop those that you lead not only into individual successes or good team members but into Leaders.

In the next chapter, we will address some of the practical application of the S in BAMCIS when we discuss how to Watch and Learn.

SECTION 3: TACTICS, TECHNIQUES, AND PROCEDURES

Chapter 8: The "S" in BAMCIS

"We manage things. We lead people." -- Hamda Khan

EMPO(W)ER: Watch and Learn

In the last chapter, we discussed the importance of optimizing your environment for growth so that you could use mistakes and failures by your team as opportunities to grow, learn, and build trust (both yours and your team's) in your process and your systems. In this chapter, we will go into a bit more detail about how to do that, about how to master that critical sixth step, the S in BAMCIS, how to master Supervising the execution of your plans. There are a couple of points that we will focus on in this chapter, and though we will deal with them individually, I wanted you to keep in mind the fact that they are all connected. Collectively, they embody what we mean when we say supervise. These are the tactics, techniques, and procedures that will help you to make your strategy successful and bring your visions to fruition.

- Trust Your Team
- Trust the Process
- Build Trust in the Process
- Inspect What you Expect
- Measure What's Important
- Accentuate the Positive

Protect Your Team from Catastrophic Failures

Trust Your Team:

It is imperative that once you have given your team their roles and responsibilities that you trust them to accomplish the task. Much of the work that we did in the earlier chapters was to allow you the freedom to do just that. As we have discussed, you communicate in both verbal and nonverbal ways to your team. Some of this communication is even unconscious.

Have you ever left a meeting with someone where they said all the right things, but you just had a gut feeling that you weren't going to be awarded the project or the promotion? That is because your subconscious mind is capable of receiving 100 times more signals than your conscious mind is able to process. You were picking up on the cues in body language, tone, etc. that the person was giving that told you that there was incongruence in what they were saying and what was true. You may not have understood why you had that gut feeling, but you just knew that they didn't trust you, believe in you, or want to promote you.

Your communication with your people is the same, and they can read your trust in them the same way. This is why we focus so much on their strengths; this is why we evaluate our expectations. We want all of our communication with our team to be authentic and congruent with our belief about what will happen. Congruent communication is the ultimate strategy for Empowering Leadership. Trusting your team is one way we ensure that our communication is congruent.

Like I said before, this isn't some positive mental attitude discussion. This is really and truly getting yourself to a place where you can trust and believe in your people because you have done the work necessary to set them up for success. If you trust them, your people will know, and it will help them to trust themselves more. In many ways, as an Empowering Leader, you are the first follower for those that you are developing into leaders. You are the first one to believe that they are capable and who is willing to trust them to lead. Trusting your team is the foundation of building them into the leaders that they are supposed to be.

Trust the Process:

Similarly, it is imperative that you trust the process. One of the points that we learned during Marine Corps Officer training is how important your beliefs are to your troops. During the bleak times, when they don't believe in themselves or their mission, they look to their leader as a source of inspiration and comfort. As the leader, you are the rock, you are the steady hand, you are the North Star for your team. That is why so much of the planning process is focused on what the leader can do to develop a plan that the leader can believe in; because during the execution phase, the leader has to maintain faith and fidelity in what the team is doing. Otherwise the whole enterprise crumbles.

Therefore, during the execution phase of your plan, when your people have been released to accomplish their tasks, it is imperative that you trust the process and that they know that you trust the process. They must know that you believe, even when they don't, and that the team will reach the finish line. This will convince them to work harder and do more than they would have done based off of their belief alone.

Building Trust In the Process:

So, of course, this begs the question, "What to do if you don't trust the process?" Examine and Evaluate your Expectations.

There is a difference between trusting the process to be perfect and trusting the process to deliver the results you need. One of my favorite parts of the Constitution is in the Preamble. It is in the first line where it says,

"We the People, in order to form a MORE PERFECT UNION…"

The thing that they knew, even then, at the most idealistic of times in American history and possibly the history of the world, was to evaluate their own expectations. They could have come out and declared that they were going to form the most awesome nation the world had ever known (I'm sure that some of them were thinking it). But no, they set the bar high but attainable. They decreed the purpose was to form a more perfect union. There again is Aspiration popping up.

And it is an important point to learn that your process is never going to be perfect. You are always going to be learning because you are always going to be growing as a leader and your team will always be growing as a team. Your goal, therefore, is not to strive for perfection but rather for progress. When you continue to progress, you can excel. With that goal in mind, here are some practical steps you can take that will allow you to constantly improve your team and your process. The great part about having this understanding is that the more you use the following tools, the more you reinforce your belief and your team's belief in the process.

***

This next story is an example of what the process of this change looks like in real life. As a Jiu Jitsu instructor, when I first began, I always wanted my students to be able to feel completely confident in their abilities to defend themselves. This was because my first students were my wife and daughter (my son was just one at the time, so thankfully, he never got to have me as a bad instructor). Initially, I would agonize over them getting the move right because I wanted them to be able to defend themselves against everything. I wanted to get them there as quickly as possible. I wanted them to be safe. This went on for two years and got bad enough that my wife didn't really like training with me. She would actually actively avoid it (luckily, my daughter was only five, so she just liked playing with Daddy, but I could tell she didn't like it as much as when we began). In the end, what I was communicating to them was that I wasn't confident in the path that they were on. I was afraid of their failure, and they could feel that. That just exacerbated their own fears, especially my wife's.

When I studied to become a Certified Gracie Jiu Jitsu Instructor, one of the main things that we talked about in the training was trusting the system. My instructors reframed the goal for me, and it allowed me to realize that if I just did my job then the system would take care of the rest. Since then, I have been able to help countless men, women, and children learn how to defend themselves in much less time than it took with my family (and they were much happier along the way).

Coincidentally, after I started training to become an instructor, I reengaged my wife and my daughter (and my son, he was four at time I became an instructor), and they have all developed a love for Jiu Jitsu. They also began to grow and develop faster than I had ever imagined, especially my wife. I am now confident that she can defend herself, and she actually likes doing Jiu Jitsu with me. Moral of the story is: You have to trust the system in order to make it work.

Do not underestimate what you can accomplish through reshaping and keeping fidelity with your process. The preliminary steps discussed in the Vision and Strategy sections will help you to relieve the unreasonable standards that you are holding yourself to and your team to. They will allow you to be comfortable with not being perfect and to build the resilience that you need to keep growing. Remember: This is the foundation for greatness. Doing this will also help you to set up short-term, mid-term, and long-term goals that are actually achievable. This reframing will alleviate most of the pressure to do everything now.

Inspect What You Expect

The first point is pretty simple. My father, a former drill sergeant in the Army, used to say this to me all the time as a kid. It was like déjà vu when I became a Marine officer and heard it all the time. In the military, we have inspections constantly. Inspections before a field training op, room inspections when we get back, vehicle inspections before liberty, administrative inspections. The list goes on and on. Many people don't understand the purpose of these inspections. They feel like they are intrusive and demeaning. And so when they get to a place of leadership, they decide that they are not going to inspect so much. And this is always a disaster.

The reason why is that inspections have two critical components that improve performance. The first we discussed in the last chapter when we talked about QC checks. Having inspections allows you to use the time as an opportunity for feedback and trust building. If used correctly, you as the leader get more opportunities to catch your people doing the right thing, and your people have more opportunities to interact with you in a safe setting. The other reason that inspections are critical is that they serve as reinforcing communication to everyone of what the priorities are for the team.

Have you ever noticed that your team seems to perform better on the things that they know you are going to inspect? Reports, presentations, memos, things that they know will get read and will have some impact on their salary or promotion status seem to be turned in on time and done well. Things like showing up on time or following up on an item that you have forgotten about for two weeks seem to not get on their radar.

We like to think that this is because they are lazy or not paying attention. However, your people are much smarter than you give them credit for. They know that in an environment where they may not feel like they have time to do everything it makes the most sense to do the things that are paid attention to. Though this may seem like a problem, this is actually tremendously helpful to you and can be a powerful asset in your quest to improve your team's productivity.

While it requires a bit more forethought, (which you may have noticed by now is a theme throughout this process) the payoff is tremendous. By being consistent in your communication about what is important you have the ability to motivate your team simply by doing your job. No extra work necessary. The things you pay attention to, they will pay attention to. The things you ask questions about, they will ask questions about. The things you inspect will show what you expect, and they will get done. Your team will rise to meet your expectations; they simply need your communication about them to be congruent.

Measure What Is Important

Achieving congruence in the communication of your expectations is a function of measurement. It is nearly impossible to inspect something if you have not clearly defined what you want and determined how you will measure it beforehand. One of the reasons that you want to focus so heavily on the SMART goals process and, more specifically, the measurement part of this process is that it facilitates your ability to properly plan, delegate, and supervise. The clarity that you achieve using this process affects all of the ways that you implement your vision and strategies with your team.

If you want to be able to build trust in the system, you have to know what you are looking for and be able to recognize it when you see it. Without determining how you are measuring success, recognizing success becomes nearly impossible and failing to do so will serve to undermine all of the progress you are making. If at any time you feel like you are having a hard time inspecting your people or conducting useful QC checks, that is a sign that your clarity is off, and you need to re-address the Clarity of your SMART Goals.

Accentuate the Positive

Many people believe that supervision is about pointing out the areas for improvement. While part of your job as the team leader is to protect your team from catastrophic failures, this actually represents a very small part of what you do when you are supervising. The majority of what you do when you are supervising/facilitating is being the cheerleader for your team. You have to remember that the reason that you have gotten to this place in your plan is that you have laid the groundwork for them to be successful.

You have examined your team and know their strengths. You have evaluated your expectations and made sure they were reasonable. You have defined success for them in a way that set them up to succeed. You have established roles, issued tasks, and empowered your team to accomplish those tasks. And you have optimized your environment for growth so as to provide ample opportunities for feedback, course correction, and assistance if it is needed. You have put them in the best position to maximize their capabilities.

As I mentioned earlier, if you are going to show them that you trust the them and the system, then your job is to be the first follower and to be the best cheerleader you can be. You are to believe in and root for their success more than anyone else. That doesn't mean that you don't see when they make mistakes; it simply means that the mistakes are not your sole focus. Unless their mistakes are in the category that I address in the next section, there is no need now for you to deal with them right now. Make note of them and then focus on whatever positive thing you see that you want them to continue doing.

Protect Your Team from Catastrophic Failures

As I said, accentuating the positive is the order of the day. The supervisor is the head cheerleader for the team during the execution phase of the plan. However, there are times where the team is headed for a catastrophic failure, and as the Leader, you must step in and protect them. Understand, however, that your goal is not to protect them from the failure itself (because failure is just another learning opportunity). Your goal is to protect them from the finality of the failure and from the repercussions of the failure that they are not ready to handle.

The issue that will be addressed up front in this section is how we define catastrophic failure. This definition will and should change as you continue working with your team. More importantly, your definition of catastrophic failure should always be viewed from this perspective: What is something that can happen, the results of which neither my team nor I have developed the resiliency to recover from?

Here's why this perspective is so important: There are certain things that you just don't bounce back from. It's not that you can't, but if you are not ready, you won't.

Much of the research on Post Traumatic Stress Disorder (PTSD) centers on this fact. The issue is not the trauma; we all suffer and recover from trauma every day of our lives. From bee stings to assaults to incarceration and genocide, there are people all over the world who have endured tremendous suffering and do not suffer from PTSD. The distinguishing factor of those who suffer from PTSD is not the trauma that they suffer but rather their mind's ability to bounce back from that trauma. The mind's ability to return to a state of normalcy. For many people that suffer from PTSD, they have had their reality torn in such a way that repairing it is very difficult and feels impossible.

Now, those things are different for everyone, and they change over the course of our lifetimes. However, it would be irresponsible of me to send you on this journey and not prepare you for the fact that there are certain things that your team will not be able to do. There are certain things that your positive attitude and your belief in their ability will not be able to overcome. Thankfully, as a society we have begun to appreciate and study PTSD in a serious way. There is a lot of work being done by the academic and professional counseling communities that is helping those who suffer from PTSD improve their resiliency and their sense of peace and control in their lives. While it is great that people can recover from these types of experiences, as leaders, it is imperative that we are aware of the potential for this type of shock for those we lead and prepare them for it. That is the purpose of this section.

I want you to understand that these are not absolute circumstances and, over time, they will occur less and less. But, if you are reading this book, you are likely in a place where your team is doing things that could get them or you fired. And the truth is that you can't get better if you don't have a team or a company to lead.

So what qualifies as a catastrophic failure? Here are a few examples.

Between a Rock and a Hard Place:

It is important that you protect your people from being placed in situations where they can't win. As a Company Commander, I had enlisted and senior enlisted members who worked on my staff. However, in our company – we had other officers even some who outranked me – that we were responsible for and had to interact with on a daily basis. Now, I had positional authority; I was in charge, but in the grand scheme of things, those officers outranked me and my staff. At times, they would attempt to get my staff to do things that I had explicitly told them not to do. This put my staff in a weird place that they could not resolve comfortably on their own. If they told the officers no and I didn't stand by them, they would lose face. Their reputation, and possibly their careers, would be harmed. Adding to this problem is the fact that they might have to work for these officers in a different capacity in the future.

      Recognizing this, I made sure that I cleared the way for my staff to do what they needed to do. I made sure that everyone in the company knew that the only person who could change an order that I gave was me or my direct boss, the battalion commander. If the order wasn't coming from either of us, then my staff had my permission, and my authority, to have the person who had a problem deal directly with me. By backing their position, I removed their concern about getting in trouble or doing the wrong thing. I simply took that off of their plates. At the same time, I increased their respect for me, their trust in me, and their belief that I would take care of them. They trusted me, and they trusted the system to set them up for success. This is what must be done for our teams.

System Malfunction:

Sometimes you see that someone is not going to be successful at something because of an error you made in selecting them for this responsibility, or you realize that the process that you set up has some sort of major flaw. This is the time where you must step up and take responsibility for your part. You step in and take the project back, or you work with your team to improve it, but you remain clear at all times that you are doing this because of something that you failed to do and not because they are failing. You must see these processes from the perspective of what you could have done better to set your team up for success.

It's not Me, it's You!

On rare occasions, your people will fail because of some intractable problem that they have. Perhaps they have decided that they no longer want to work on your team, or perhaps there is some irreparable rift that occurred long before you started working on improving your team dynamics with the EMPOWER Method, and they just can't move forward. In these instances, it is incumbent on you as the leader to ensure that you send these people on their way. Keeping them around only serves to damage the team dynamic and to wear on you as the leader. Additionally, keeping them around will wear on your team members who are trying to do what you have asked. The next section focuses on all the tools that you have at your disposal to ensure that you have created an environment where termination, if necessary, can be done efficiently, effectively, and with the smallest amount of disruption to your team. (For a detailed discussion of termination, see Chapter 11).

***

One final note about protecting your team. Internalize this mantra: If it's good, it is them. If it's bad, it's you!

If your people are responsible in small or in large part for your success, it is imperative that you make sure they receive the recognition they deserve. At meetings, at gatherings, as often as you can, you as the leader must ensure that you are championing the cause of your people. This includes recommending them for promotions rather than hoarding their talents on your team. Remember: Your goal as an Empowering Leader is to create other leaders, not to stunt people's growth so that you can have the best team.

Be Consistent with Your Reporting and Meeting Schedules

The final way that you build trust in the system is by building consistency into it. It is important that your people have the comfort of knowing that they can communicate with you regularly. Here are a few suggestions.

Weekly Meetings:

One way to make this happen is to schedule regular meetings with your people. I am a fan of short weekly meetings; however, you can meet more or less often if that is better for your environment. I would not recommend meeting less than one time per week unless you don't work with your team on a daily basis. If you have an arrangement where you don't, I would at least recommend that you send your team weekly updates, even if you are not going to see them.

These meetings must have an agenda and a time limit. The purpose of these meetings is not to hash out everything that you haven't discussed or to ruminate on what you think the team should or shouldn't be doing. They have the purpose of giving your people opportunities to update you on what they are doing and to ask your input on anything they are struggling with. They are set up for you to be able to get an idea of where you are needed and how you can help. These meetings are inspections. You can use these meetings as extra QC checks. They help you know if your people are progressing at the rate that you would like them to.

Monthly/Quarterly/Semi-Annual/Annual Progress Reviews:

Another idea is the Progress Review/Evaluation meeting. These should be held as frequently as you believe is necessary depending on the members of your team. If you haven't worked with your team members for more than a year through this process, I would recommend ensuring that at the very least you do quarterly reviews. Monthly reviews are preferred until there is a significant amount of trust built up between the parties. These reviews are formal instances where you sit down with your team members individually, and you review their progress and your expectations for them.

You want to always begin these meetings with a review of the positive improvements that you have noticed in their performance. This sets the tone for the meeting. Next you want to have them review with you their evaluation of their progress on the items that were the focus for this reporting period. Finally, you want to work with them to develop a plan to improve on the areas where they need to improve.

Reports:

There are a number of common things that your people turn in on a weekly or monthly basis. You want to ensure that these reporting periods coincide with your meetings so that there is time built into the schedule to clear up any communication inconsistencies. Too often we lose time having extra meetings which last ten or fifteen (or thirty) minutes to clarify things that could be easily reviewed in a one to two minute report brief during a regularly scheduled meeting. Utilizing our meetings to deal with these issues does two things:

1. It saves us time having to do this work in multiple meetings.

2. It increases the positive peer pressure to perform.

No one wants to be the only one at the meeting that isn't prepared. Therefore, just by the way that you structure your reporting, you improve the quality of that reporting. On a side note: If you have a majority of your people reporting poorly in the meeting or you feel like the same information is consistently missing from multiple reports, then you have the feedback that you need to identify the problem in the system. You must realize that it is likely the reporting process and not the people that is the problem. This is something that you might not catch if they are all reporting individually or by email at various times throughout the week.

***

The execution process of your plan is the time for you to be a fan of your team. I titled this step Watch and Learn because that is mostly what you do here. For the most part, you are a silent observer, marveling at the abilities of your team and appreciating all of the work that you don't have to do because they are capable of accomplishing it. When you are needed to intervene, you are a willing participant, however much of your work has already been accomplished. This is the space the Empowering Leader seeks to occupy more and more of the time. Mastering this step is the first step to becoming a Legacy Leader and getting your people to say, in the words of Lao Tzu, "We Did It Ourselves!"

Chapter 9: You Don't Want to Have All the Answers

EMPOW(E)R: Engage Their Inner Problem Solver

So far you have learned how to develop the Leader's Mind and the tools in the Leader's Toolkit that allow you to get your team to the point where they can accomplish great things. By Evaluating your Expectations, Measuring their Expectations, Playing to Win with Proper Delegation, Optimizing your Timelines, and Watching and Learning, you have built up your trust in your team and your process to get the job done; you have cultivated their trust in themselves, in you, and in your project; you have given them clarity over what their roles are and how they can know when they are doing what they are supposed to do and when they need improvement; you have set up feedback opportunities for them while they are working on the project, and you have been there when they needed you to help them manifest the greatness that lies within them so that they could do their best work.

If you to stop right there, you would have already improved your leadership style by leaps and bounds. You would be well on your way to being a great coach, a great team leader. However, that is not the goal. As you can see this process is very intensive. It adds a lot of thinking and preparing to your plate. If you were to try to continue to work by only improving your abilities you would have a ceiling to your productivity and that of your team because you can only lead so many people in a day. There is only so much of you that can go around.

This reality and the solution to this problem is what makes Legacy Leaders so different from other types of leaders. Legacy Leaders understand this situation and don't see it as an obstacle but rather as the true purpose of the journey. Remember: The ultimate purpose of the Legacy Leader is not to get things done. It's not even to help others become great Do-ers. The purpose of the Legacy Leader is to create other Empowering Leaders. The final two steps of this process set the stage for your ultimate transformation from an Empowering Leader to a Legacy Leader. These tactics will become your strategy as you move further and further along the Leader's Way.

Engaging Their Inner Problem-Solver

So how does engaging their inner problem-solver help your team to learn to be more productive and take more initiative? It does this by teaching them to think like a leader. To be a problem-solver rather than a problem-spotter. Throughout this book, I have told you that feedback loops are of vital importance to your processes as a leader. They are necessary to cultivate and develop trust between you and your team, and they are necessary to develop your team's trust in their abilities and your process. This final step is designed to help them develop trust in their own processes and abilities. And that is why, in this section, you are the facilitator of their reflection, rather than the giver of wisdom. You must approach this stage of their learning with the care and compassion of empathy. You must always keep in mind what they are going through and how they are thinking and feeling as they are making this journey. Remember: This is the beginning of their development as well. The budding of their Leader's Heart and Mind.

The tactic for ushering your people from problem-spotters to problem-solvers is the Socratic Method.

"The oldest, and still the most powerful, teaching tactic for fostering critical thinking is Socratic teaching. Socratic teaching focus on giving students questions, not answers. We model an inquiring, probing mind by continually probing into the subject with questions."

Paul, R. and Elder, L. (April 1997). Foundation for Critical Thinking

This tactic will be employed during specific meetings where the conditions have been set for maximum effectiveness. These are any meetings designed for reviewing performance after the fact.

In the last chapter, I explained the need for you to make notes of the things that your people may have missed that were not catastrophic failures. I emphasized that these didn't need to be pointed out right away. Also discussed, in the Evaluate Your

Expectations chapter, was the need to pay attention to your team's weaknesses and to keep a list of things that you want to improve on. The purpose of you writing them down and planning when you use them is so that you can maximize the effect of the work you do on them. Now let's discuss how to deal with these what I call Teachable Moments.

You can use this tactic with many of the tools that you have already learned in the process (QC checks, performance reviews, weekly/monthly meetings, impromptu conversations, etc.). However, the main tool that you want to use for this is a critical review as a group of the team's performance after the fact. In the Marine Corps, we would do what we call debriefings, after action reports, and lessons learned. These were times where we would report on what had occurred, what went right, what could have gone better, and what failed. We would look at the situation from the vantage point of 20/20 hindsight, and we would distinguish between the things that were simply mistakes and the things that needed systems or rules implemented to reduce the likelihood of their occurrence in the future.

You should have this time built into your schedule at least monthly. More important than the meetings with your team is the manner in which you conduct the meetings. It is imperative that you are not doing the majority of the talking. You are leading the session, but you are leading it by engaging your group and facilitating their discovery of what will work best for them.

Paul and Elder, in their work, explain that the goal of the facilitator is to "act as the logical equivalent of the inner critical voice which the mind develops when it develops critical thinking abilities." While you don't have pre-planned answers that you want your people to regurgitate, you do have a direction that you want them to go. Remember, this is a learning process for you as well. "By following up all answers with further questions, and by selecting questions which advance the discussion, the Socratic questioner forces [their team] to think in a disciplined, intellectually responsible manner, while continually aiding [the team members] by posing facilitating questions."

In this way, you are teaching them to think critically about the issues you recognized and helping them to develop their proficiency at coming up with solutions on their own. You are teaching them to think like a problem solver. You are teaching them to think like a leader.

This is imperative if you want to disrupt the pattern that already exists where they mess up and come to you to fix it. There is a fascinating article that discusses this in the Harvard Business review called, "Whose Monkey Is It Anyway?" I highly recommend that you read that article to give you even more insight into the type of interactions that you want to have with the members of your team regarding challenges and finding solutions.

Measurement is Critical

Here I must reiterate the importance of measurement. It is critical that you be prepared with facts when you facilitate these discussions. When you are working with your team you want to ensure that you create a safe space for them to explore but that you also facilitate a discussion that can have an actual destination. The goal here is not just to teach them how to think; it is to teach them how to problem-solve. They actually have to leave the session with solutions or at least a roadmap to find solutions.

And you do too. These sessions are as much about you learning what works for your team and what doesn't as they are about them learning how to overcome future obstacles. At all times, you are looking at the system and determining what needs to be tweaked or changed to better serve your people. Remember: The tasks are going to get done; that's the easy part. Your focus is how can you be the best at taking care of your people so that they can do the tasks to the best of their abilities. While they are focusing on how to get better at the tasks, you are focusing on improving your processes.

Both of these results are much more difficult to arrive at if you cannot reference any measurable benchmarks. If you remember our discussion about SMART goal-setting and the need for measurement, the same is true here. You can only improve your processes if you can define what improvement is. Therefore, it is incumbent upon you as the leader to enter the meeting with an idea of where you are and what direction you want to go. To do that you must have data. Measurement is critical!

The secret to getting your team to take inspired action and anticipate next steps

By Engaging Their Inner Problem-Solver, you begin step-by-step, day-by-day, to work yourself out of a job. As you teach your team how to think about problems and, more importantly, as they begin to see themselves solving the problems, they come to rely on you less and less. You will see that they will not even wait until these sessions to spot and solve problems. These sessions will occur with less frequency as they are replaced with briefings to you on how they have already fixed their problems.

This, coupled with the work that you have done in the previous steps to build their trust in you, to create a safe environment, to protect them from catastrophic failure, and to change the way they relate failure and success, will make your team more comfortable with working outside of the permission boxes that they have lived in for so much of their lives.

They will begin to trust themselves to do the job well. They will take the inspired action that comes to them when they see something that they can solve. They will also anticipate the next steps you would want them to take because they have worked with you enough and developed their critical thinking skills enough that they can have confidence that they are seeing the problem the way that you do or at least in a way that is congruent with your team's values and vision.

Step-by-step, day-by-day, your team will be able to take over the duties of managing their own performance and even managing the performance of other junior team members. As you continue to implement your system, your people will begin to manifest the greatness that lies within them. You will begin to have your reasons for hiring them or keeping them on your team confirmed again and again.

And the awesome part about this is that once they are empowered, once they are liberated from the fear of failure and emboldened by the confidence of trust, they will begin to surprise you on the regular by accomplishing things that, while congruent with your vision, are beyond anything that you could have even dreamed of. This is the point at which the synergy begins.

Chapter 10: You Get More of What You Focus On

> *"When we notice others making suboptimal decisions, we automatically fast forward in our heads and visualize their failure, leading us to warn them about the devastation we envision. But what the research here suggests is that we need to consciously overcome our habit of trying to scare people into action, and instead highlight the rewards that come with reaching our goals."* –Tali Sharot, HBR article (https://hbr.org/2017/09/what-motivates-employees-more-rewards-or-punishments)

EMPOWE(R): Reward What You Want to Continue

As I mentioned before, you have tools in your toolbox that will help your team learn to be more productive, take more initiative, engage their inner problem solver, and ultimately take ownership of their performance and their results. This is what maximizes your effectiveness as a Leader. The critical point about all of this is that you are trying to get them to DO something. Just as Dr. Sharot explains in her article, we focus on trying to get our teams to avoid calamity rather than getting them to approach greatness. The distinction is subtle, I know, but it is supremely important.

And that is why this chapter comes directly after chapter nine on engaging our teams to solve problems. Understand that the purpose and goal of the EMPOWER method is not to get our teams to focus on problems or even to solve them. It's to get them to become wedded to a goal and to be so dedicated to success that they are able to overcome any obstacles in their path. Again, the focus is on achieving greatness, not avoiding calamity; winning, not avoiding losing; achieving success, not avoiding failure.

The key to the distinction is found in comparing these two questions: "What happens if things go wrong?" and "What happens if things go right?" If you remember, in the Watch and Learn chapter, I spoke to you about the need as a leader to protect your team from catastrophic failure. This is where the question "What happens if things go wrong?" comes into play. Notice that this was only one section of the book, and while it is an important section, it is important because of the role it plays in creating a safe environment for you and your people to learn and explore how to achieve success.

I want to be clear here, the governing question of your leadership journey with any group that you lead should always be, "What happens if things go right?" You should always be focusing on the positive possibilities. Everything in your systems and your processes should be implemented with the purpose of reinforcing the strengths of those on your team. Every process and system should be imbued with your hopeful optimism of the great things that you and your team are going to accomplish. Because here is the truth that you need to know as a leader: You have no idea how amazing your people can be on their best day!

That should fill you with a sense of excitement and anticipation. Again, looking at the people on your team from the analysis that you did in Step 1, what you will find is that you have been gifted with an array of individuals who have a unique set of skills and are capable of accomplishing amazing things. This is the joy of the Empowering Leader. The sky's the limit to what your team can accomplish if you can do your job right and then get out of the way.

Now the techniques and strategies that I have given you up to this point are all about doing the job right and preparing them to think and act. This chapter is about how you reinforce your systems and processes so that they produce more of what you want and less of what you don't want. In order to do that, it is imperative that you commit to modeling this truth: Positive reinforcement is better at provoking desired actions than negative reinforcement or punishment.

Now, I don't expect you to just take my word for it, so I want to present you with some evidence. I have summarized it here, since I did not intend for this book to be a scholarly endeavor; however, the wealth of scientific evidence that has been compiled by psychologists and neuroscientists on how we are best motivated to act or refrain from acting is enough to keep you busy studying it for the rest of your adult life if you are so inclined.

So, how does it apply to us as Empowering Leaders?

Well, the first thing to look at is goals. As I said earlier, you picked this book up because you wanted your team to DO something. Therefore, that has to be the guiding principle behind everything that you put in place. You want everything you do in facilitating and Leading your team to reinforce your effort to get them to take more action, be more proactive, and think more like leaders. This is why positive reinforcement is so critical to the Empowering Leader.

Note: The things that we discuss in this chapter should be implemented liberally throughout the program; however, they are especially necessary after your team has completed their work and met their goals. Why? Because this is the most powerful time to reinforce behavior that you want to continue.

In the article mentioned above, Dr. Sharot chronicles a study done in a large hospital's intensive care unit regarding employees sanitizing (washing) their hands before and after interacting with patients. Now, all of the employees had been instructed on the need to do this, and there were posters all around the hospital which indicated the dangers of not taking this action, including at all of the sanitizing stations. Additionally, these were highly trained and capable employees. We are talking doctors and nurses here.

With a highly capable staff, an environment that was set up for the staff to be successful, and plenty of information about the dangers of not taking the action, you would think that the majority would model the desired behavior. You would be wrong.

The reality, as Dr. Sharot explains, was that only about "10% of the medical staff sanitized their hands before and after entering a patient's room, [as was the hospital protocol]. This was despite the fact that the employees knew they were being recorded."

Now, let's think about this for a moment. Doctors and nurses are possibly the most knowledgeable people in world regarding the dangers of disease transmission. They understand that by not being vigilant about washing their hands they are actually making their jobs harder. They are also aware that their behavior is being monitored. Yet, they still don't do the behavior that is the best thing to do, the behavior that is communicated well to them, the behavior that they know is their job to do.

While many might instantly jump to the conclusion that they need to be reprimanded and disciplined, the evidence suggests this is not the prudent action. Discipline and reprimand are best at getting people to stop behavior that you don't want them to do. For example, "punishment can be effective in stopping undesirable employee behaviors such as tardiness, absenteeism, or substandard work performance. However, punishment does not necessarily cause an employee to demonstrate a desirable behavior." (Punishment in the workplace creates undesirable side effects, Gene Milbourn Jr., Wichita Business Journal, 1996). In situations like this, where you want someone to DO something, the evidence is clear. Positive reinforcement is the best method.

Positive reinforcement was first described by B.F. Skinner in his work on operant conditioning as the addition of a reinforcing stimulus following a particular behavior. In non-science speak, that means giving a reward for favorable behavior. The power of positive reinforcement is that it makes a behavior exponentially more likely to occur again in the future. "When a favorable outcome, event, or reward occurs after an action, that particular response or behavior will be strengthened." (Very Well Mind.com)

Positive reinforcement is important to be distinguished from negative reinforcement and punishment. Negative reinforcement is attempting to incentivize a behavior by the removal of a negative outcome if the behavior is not done. The basic idea in negative reinforcement is this: You DO something to AVOID a negative, natural consequence. For example, you are going to the beach or pool, and you put on sunscreen. When you come home, you have avoided sunburn; therefore, you are more likely to put on sunscreen in the future. For punishment (which is the addition or removal of a condition in order to weaken a behavior) the difference is that the goal is to prohibit an action, not to increase the likelihood of another one. Punishment is for things you want your people to stop doing.

Often people make mistakes in this regard and think that the negative consequences are actually strong enough to get your team to choose the right behavior. However, this gives our team and their amazing minds too little credit for complexity, nuance, and creativity. It also underestimates the difficulty of figuring out what is right to do.

"Learning from mistakes is more complex than carrying on in the same way as before. You have to ask yourself what precisely went wrong." That is, it takes more analysis to figure out what you are doing wrong and how to correct it than it does to figure out you are doing something right and keep doing it. (Rewards are Better than Punishment: Here's Why rewards are more effective than punishment--with children. Jay Belsky, Ph.D.)

This is why in this program the focus so much on developing multiple feedback loops for identifying problems and looking for solutions. It is a much more complex inquiry than the credit it gets. You may stop a negative behavior by punishment, and you can set up systems to force the intellectual consideration necessary to learn from negative reinforcement, but that doesn't guarantee that the right positive behavior will follow. Too often, leaders set up punishment regimes or assume that their team is negatively reinforced in a similar way as they are. Only later do they realize the obvious: that everyone on their team is an individual, with different strengths, different motivations, and often times a different perspective on life. This results in frustration that the systems that are set up don't produce the desired results. This is why the best and most effective way to incentivize a particular behavior is to positively reinforce it. The following is an example of my journey to this realization from my life as a parent.

Since our kids were old enough to understand that we don't have a maid, my wife and I have wanted our children to do more around the house regarding picking up after themselves. We tried a number of different methods. We made sure that we showed them how to pick up after themselves and how to do their other chores.

We chastised them when they didn't do them. We explained to them our disappointment when they didn't do them. We threatened them with punishment (and followed through) if they continued to disregard their chores. None of this worked and these methods constantly made us feel more and more distant from our children, more and more like the bad guys. Sound familiar?

My wife and I couldn't understand what was going wrong. The benefits of the children doing their chores were obvious to us, and we thought it was to them as well. Ironically, despite all of our training as educators which should have alerted us to the foolishness of our assumption, we were convinced these benefits would be obvious and powerful influences on the behavior of our children. We were right about the benefits being obvious, but boy were we wrong about them being powerful influences.

Our children complained when the house was messy just as much as we did. They understood that if we don't clean up regularly, then we have to do it for a longer time later, and that always sucks. They understood that if the dishes aren't washed and put away, then they pile up in the sink and that means that we run out of clean dishes. They knew and hated that this meant they would have to wash a dish before they eat or drink anything, and they would have to do that in a full sink. They got this on an intellectual level, but understanding these truths still didn't change their behavior. And punishment just wasn't sustainable in the long term. It meant that my wife and I would constantly have to enforce the rules and be the bad guys. Our kids were ten and six at the time that we changed our tactics. We had been working at this with little success for the better part of four years. Continuing the way we were going was an exhausting proposition. We had to find another way.

So, how did we use positive reinforcement to change this? We tied positive outcomes that were important to them to their performance of their chores. This seems simple, but it is truly profound. We ensured that when they did their chores we praised them for what they did. We also began giving them an allowance that was based on them doing their chores, instead of them simply being our children.

Similarly, we restructured our systems so that they more obviously attached the positive stimulus to the behavior. Instead of trying to get them to do their chores as an abstract concept, we just attached going outside or playing video games or watching TV to completing their chores. Therefore, every time they got their chores done, then they were free. Our standard answer to their question of can I go outside or can I play video games changed from "Yes or No" to "Are your chores done?" This did two things: 1) It gave them more agency in their own lives, and 2) it helped to reinforce the questions they needed to ask themselves to reach their goals.

Does that mean that everything is perfect now? Of course not. Did it take some time for the results to show. Yes, it did.

The important point, however, is that it took way less time to get to those results than anticipated. And here is the critical point: Not only did we dramatically improve their performance, the way we got there is sustainable and actually requires less input from us as time goes on, rather than more. Another amazing result is that our children are able to correct themselves and others. They are even able to teach others (their friends and relatives who visit the house) how to be successful in the system. They have taken ownership of their chores. My son RJ is now the person that reminds people of the rule that we only have one pair of shoes by the door. Why? Because he sees the connection between people not following the rule and an increase in his workload.

    Now, because of our system, we don't have to do much more than be consistent to ensure that chores are done. Additionally, we were able to change the dynamic in the house. Though the kids may still get angry about having to do their chores, that anger is not directed at us unless we are not putting things where they are supposed to be. We get to be the good guys. They show me or my wife that they have done their chores in anticipation of praise and reward. They come to us dressed and with chores complete when they want to go outside or have company over. They are pro-active, and they take pride in what they do. They are the owners now. They are Empowered.

    The hospital study had similar results. To effect their positive reinforcement strategy, the hospital installed an electronic board in the hallway of the unit that gave employees instant feedback. "Every time they washed their hands the board displayed a positive message (such as "Good job!") and the current shift's hand-hygiene score would go up." Over the course of one month they improved their handwashing rates "to nearly 90%." (Dr. Sharot article)

Why does this work? Because the positive feedback triggers the reward centers in the brain that are designed to help us learn what behaviors we want to keep. By rewarding what you want to continue, you utilize this evolutionary principle to promote those very behaviors that are most beneficial and increase the likelihood of your team doing them. An added benefit of this type of practice is that it is intellectually easier to understand.

On a side note, this is why for pre-adolescent children, positive reinforcement is exponentially more impactful in training them to get to the right behavior. Because it is easier to understand the connection between action and reward than it is to understand what the right thing to do is when you are simply told that what you just did was wrong, children (and adults) get to the right answer faster and with greater frequency. The logic proves the same for post-adolescents; however, we do become better equipped to gain meaning from nuance and negative reinforcement as we get older.

The fact that it is easier to understand means that your team can use their leftover brainpower to think about other, more important things like solving problems. Specifically, they have the time and the clarity to see the connections that you are not even focusing on at the time. They are then able to make decisions, not because we tell them to, but because they want to achieve their goals. This is the key benefit to infusing positive reinforcement into all of your systems and processes. You begin to remove yourself as the source of right and wrong. You begin to simply facilitate their growth rather than being necessary for their growth. This is where the true empowerment begins.

Are we eliminating any discussion of the things they mess up? No. What we are doing is ensuring that the majority of your systems and processes are set up in such a way that you incentivize what you want since the science says that you are more likely to get what you want this way. One of my mentors, Eric Thomas, puts it this way, "Where you Focus goes, your Energy flows."

The basic point is this: You get more of what you focus on.

And remember: You have plenty of things set up in your system to deal with potential threats and areas that need improvement like our systems for debriefing and reviewing our team's performance where you allow them to focus on the areas that they need to strengthen. These are all important. However, you must never lose sight of the fact that not losing, while fundamental to winning, is not sufficient to be successful. You must keep your focus and that of your team on your wins.

***

So, what are some practical things that you can do to reward your team? The answers to this question are infinite. I could write an entire book on different ways to praise your people. However, since that is not why you bought this book, let's focus on the goal of the reward, and you can determine what things work best for you. As we go forward, we will talk about praise as a type of reward; however, I will use the two terms interchangeably. As you read the rest of this chapter, keep in mind that the goal of praising/rewarding your team is to ensure that you are giving authentic praise which will trigger the reward centers of their brain to incentivize the positive behaviors you want to see in the future.

A key point about your rewards is that they must be genuine and must be based on real performance. You don't want to walk around simply giving meaningless, empty praise. Your team will see through it, and you will actually lose their trust. Similarly, you don't want to give your team rewards for things they haven't done or things that don't have anything to do with the behavior that you want them to model. If you do this, you will lose their respect.

In order for your praise to be effective, it must be something that doesn't ring hollow in the mind of the person being praised. This is why I point out again that measurement is critical. You have to know what behavior you want more of, and you need to know when your team achieves it. You have to be able to tell them exactly what they did for the praise to be authentic and effective. Remember: The goal of the praise is to trigger the reward center of the brain and tell it, "Do that again!"

I had my best training regarding praise/reward while I was studying to become a Gracie Academy Certified Instructor. One of the things that we learned was that there is no such thing as too much praise as long as it is authentic. This is because if it is authentic, then that means that the behavior is occurring. If the behavior is occurring, it deserves to be recognized. Understand that you are not doing them a favor; you are paying a debt with that praise. They have earned it.

Another key point we learned is that praise of one team member also serves to positively reinforce other team members. Therefore, praise should be done in public as much as possible. By doing so, you both reinforce the behavior that you want to continue as well as the idea that you as the leader are really paying attention. This builds trust in you (that you really care as much as you say you do) and also trust in your system (that it does give the results that you said it would). In this way you reinforce the entire process every time you reward any member on your team.

You can reward your team each time they meet a particular goal. You can reward your team when they finish a project. You can reward your team when they fail on an assignment but their performance is an improvement from their previous performance. Or when they see something that you didn't even think about. Or when they help another teammate without being asked. The possibilities are literally endless.

You want this to be the fun part of leadership. You want to enjoy giving the rewards as much as your people enjoy receiving them. You want the reward step to be a positive reinforcement for you as well. That is what will make you keep doing it. So don't pick things that you don't like. Find ways that are authentic to you. Find times and methods that will make you smile. Remember: Leadership is supposed to be fun.

Your rewards don't always have to be show-stopping affairs. Remember the hospital example. They simply saw a "Good Job" flash on a board after they did the action. As a Jiu Jitsu instructor, I would name the specific aspect of the move that someone was doing correctly and add, "Awesome!" or "Great!" to the description. This is not rocket science, although it is science. The basic idea is that you want to develop the habit of catching your people doing what you want them to do and to make it a point to let them know that you recognize it.

    This is the reason that you need to infuse each stage of the process with rewards. You want your team to constantly be receiving reinforcement about the behaviors that you want to incentivize. This is truly the skill that, once mastered, will allow you to dramatically improve performance and develop the leader in anyone. By creating systems that equip them with the Leader's Heart, Mind, and Toolkit, and by positively reinforcing their growth along the Leader's Path, you exponentially reduce their learning curve while at the same time increasing their productivity and effectiveness as team members and as future leaders. Authentic praise is the secret sauce that helps your people learn to fish, to become great at fishing, and at the same time develop their skills at teaching fishing to others. Mastering this skill is the final piece to become the type of leader that creates other leaders.

Chapter 11: Simple Does Not Equal Easy

"If it were easy, everyone would be doing it."—Every Success Coach/Motivational Speaker/Teacher/Parent Everywhere Most Notably, Dr. Eric Thomas

Obstacles, Pitfalls, and Worst-Case Scenarios

Now it would be wrong of me to give you all of this information and then send you on your way as if you now have all you need in order to overcome any obstacle that you might encounter on your path to becoming an Empowering Leader. While it would be true, you would have all the information that you need, I would be setting you out like a lamb to the slaughter. And in a book about Empowering Leadership, it's important that I lead by example. This chapter is intended to set you up for success as much as I possibly can.

Find a Mentor

One of the most important points about Empowering Leadership is that everyone along the path to becoming the type of Leader that creates other Leaders needs to have a safe space. You are going to make mistakes. You are going to mess up. You are going to fail. Knowing that is great intellectually, but it just helps tremendously to have someone there, in those times of failing and struggle, who has been where you are trying to go. Someone who can help you battle the voices of doubt and fear that will show up as soon as things don't work out exactly like you planned.

I promise you that you are going to go forward, and then when you think that you have done everything right, one of your people is going to have something slip through the cracks. Or you are going to see where you really weren't prepared enough for the project, you set them up for failure, and you have to deal with repairing a loss of trust. You are going to get overwhelmed by everything and feel like you have to change and get better all at once. That is where a mentor comes in. As you read through the situations that you see below, just remember that there is help available. While each of the following scenarios may seem daunting to overcome on your own, having a mentor who can guide you will greatly improve your results and your likelihood of success.

When you find yourself in these times, remember that you have help. You have me. I have created a seven-part video series that outlines the principles that we discuss in this book. It is free to you as my thank you for reading this book and embarking on this great journey of Legacy Leadership. Just go to **https://www.facebook.com/groups/LegacyLeaders2018/** to get access.

The next thing that I want to talk about are the two shifts that must take place in order for you to actually make this evolution. You must change your paradigm, and you must examine your communication.

Paradigm

I felt it important to reemphasize this issue one more time now that you have seen the entire program and are going to soon be employing it. How you approach your role as Leader is everything. The trust that you cultivate, the faith that you demonstrate, and the care that you show for your people is the defining factor of your leadership journey. Leadership is about relationships, not accomplishments. Your ability to trust the system and your people enough to relax your focus on the overall objective is crucial.

You must develop systems that will produce the result you want and then set your people up to perform at their maximum capability levels in those systems. Your systems are set up to maximize your people, not the other way around. Do not try to force your people to be good at a system that doesn't suit them. You must show your people that they are what is important, and you must also focus your efforts on removing yourself from the responsibility of doing tasks one after the other.

Poor Communication:

I want to spend a bit of time here discussing communication and its potential to either greatly benefit or severely hinder your efforts. Throughout all of the steps of this program, you are developing your ability to communicate with yourself, your team, your superiors, and others. Communication is at the heart of what you must do as a leader.

When I was interviewing my former first sergeant (my senior enlisted advisor from when I was commander of Bravo Company) in preparation for writing this book, one of the main things that he indicated he took from our time together was that communication and trust were key.

Now a sergeant major, he told me that the one thing that he tries to ensure all the Leaders that he mentors and advises understand is how important it is to have open and clear communication in an organization. This is what he indicated that he learned during our time together. While he always understood that you needed to communicate and you needed to earn the trust of your people, he could see during our time how much you can develop tremendous amounts of trust simply from the ways in which you communicate. You build trust when you show compassion and care for your people and impress upon them that they are important to you. You do this inherently when you strive to ensure that your communication is clear and thorough.

I thought it only fitting that I should give you the background that helped me develop this understanding of the communication process. This is something I learned at the beginning of my Leadership journey, and it has helped me every step along the way. And in true Legacy Leadership fashion, the leaders that I have helped develop are now helping those that they lead to understand it. I hope that you truly embrace the importance of this idea and apply this information to everything that we have discussed thus far about how to communicate to your people.

When I was in undergrad, I earned one of my bachelor's degrees in speech communications. The class that I believe had the most impact on me and my career was Speech Comm 230: Interpersonal Communication. This class introduced me to communication analysis, and it truly changed my life. You see, before I took this class, I believed, like most people, that communication was mostly about the transmission and receipt of messages. To be a good communicator, I believed if I simply mastered speaking and listening skills, then I would be an excellent communicator. What this class taught me was that there is so much more to communication. Since most of us are unaware of these other parts, we give them little attention, and therefore, we are often very mistaken about the actual causes of miscommunication.

While we focus on the speaking and listening when we generally think of communication, there are actually four areas of communication and eight parts to the cycle. (See Diagram on next page)

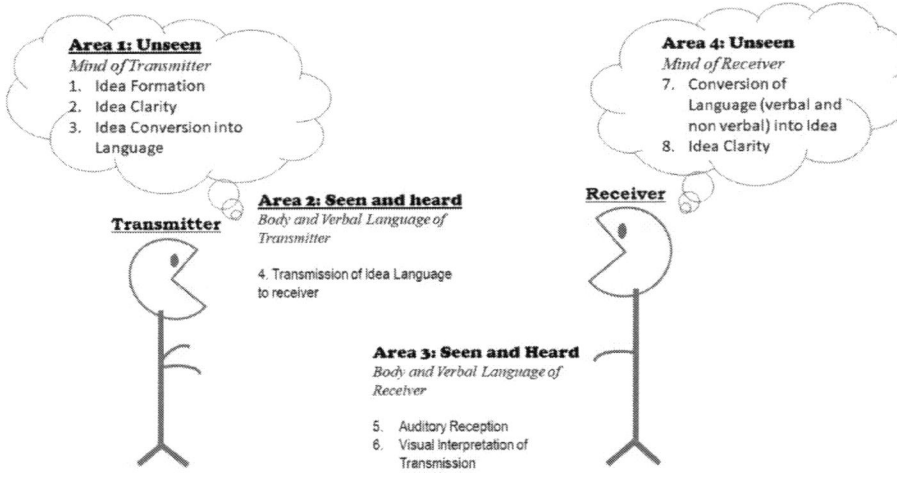

As you can see, the process goes like this:

Area 1: Mind of Communicator (Unseen)

    1.   Idea Formation

    2.   Idea Clarity

    3.   Idea Conversion into Language (Verbal and Non-Verbal, Conscious and Unconscious)

Area 2: Body of Communicator (Seen)

    4.   Transmission of Idea Language

Area 3: Body of Receiver (Seen)

    5.   Reception

    6.   Visual Interpretation of Transmission

Area 4: Mind of Receiver (Unseen)

    7.   Conversion of Language into Idea

    8.   Idea Clarity

At any point along the way, if one of the processes does not function properly, miscommunication will happen. This is why we must be good at a number of skills that have to do with communicating with and being aware of ourselves. We also have to be able to diagnose problems with the receiver that we are unable to perceive through traditional communication means (often times the receiver will not come out and say the problem or even be able to diagnose it for us). As you can see, being a good communicator involves a number of skills that are not generally taught in your public speaking courses.

If we want to have good communication with those we lead, we must understand the potential problems that lie along the path and develop feedback tools to address them. We must become skilled in diagnosing and remedying miscommunication. We must realize that miscommunication is the norm, not the anomaly. We must ensure that our systems have built in tolerances to account for the eventuality of miscommunication rather than relying on perfect communication of ideas for proper execution. The most prevalent problems happen before the idea is even presented to others. These are the issues that I generally work with my clients on because they become exponentially easier to fix with the help of an outside observer. I will outline some of these scenarios for you here. However, I highly recommend that you find a mentor to help you diagnose and address any communication issues.

If you want a more detailed discussion, you can find one in my video series, The Process. Go to https://www.facebook.com/groups/LegacyLeaders2018/ for access.

Pre-Transmission Problems:

Let's look at the first transition from Idea Formation to Idea Clarity. We can see that communication begins with idea formulation and how we communicate to ourselves about that idea greatly impacts our clarity of the idea. Many people skip this step altogether just as we discussed (See Chapter 7, the section on SMART goal setting). As I explained, specificity and clarity are extremely important in getting buy in for your vision. So before you move on to communicating with others, it is tremendously important to make sure you are communicating this way with yourself. That is why we focus so much on it in the step one.

You must always know answers to questions like: Is the idea clear or fuzzy? Do I have clarity on that idea or not?

If there is no clarity, then it will be very difficult to communicate that idea to others. Even if you do all of the other steps in the communication process correctly, at the end of the day your team will not truly understand what you want if you don't have clarity yourself.

Now, does that mean that you never talk to your team unless you are absolutely clear on what you want? Of course not! You would rarely talk to them if that were the case. The main point here is that the less clarity you have on your ideas, the more reasonable your expectations should be regarding your team's ability to do what you want. The less clear you are, the more leeway you should give yourself and your team in figuring out what "right" looks like.

Similarly, if you don't have clarity on exactly what you want, then success should be defined in a way that reflects that reality. One of my favorite examples of this is Thomas Edison's response to a reporter when the reporter asked about his team's many unsuccessful attempts at creating a sustainable incandescent light bulb. The reporter asked, "How does it feel to have failed over 1000 times to make a light bulb?" Edison replied. "We didn't fail over 1000 times; we found 1000 materials that didn't work!"

Clarity to Conversion:

Additionally, we must look at the transition between idea clarity and idea conversion into language. We must ask ourselves genuinely, "Do I have the ability to communicate about this goal to myself and others?" Have you ever had one of those moments where you have an idea, but you don't have the words to express it, or where you see someone's face but you can't remember their name? We often have the same issue with the goals we set for our teams. We know what we want but we can't seem to find the words that correctly describe it. Or, even worse, we use the wrong words to describe something. This is generally explained away with a, "Well, you know what I mean…"

As an Empowering Leader, you must be responsible for what you communicate to your team. You can never expect them to read your mind. Instead, focus on the tools that we discussed in the Engaging Their Inner Problem Solver chapter to help them think like you. Also, focus on using the tools that we discussed like the SMART goal setting and SWOT Analysis to ensure that your communication has the proper elements for your people to understand. You will get better results that way.

Transmission Issues, Receiver Issues, and Other Contributors to Miscommunication:

Many of the transmission/receiver problems related to the transmission, receipt, interpretation, and ultimately gaining meaning from your message, we have discussed already in the other chapters of the book. I have shown you how to set up systems that will maximize your team's ability to think like you think and solve problems in a way that will be successful without having to rely on you. I have also shown you how to prime the pump, so to speak, by being clear on the messages that you are communicating in your tone, body language, your thoughts and energies, along with the words that you actually use with your team. In this next section, I want to address the final piece of that puzzle: the feedback loop.

Communicating is, at all times, a two-way street. It is important to remember that being present in the moment and listening while you communicate are imperative. Your team will often give you non-verbal cues of miscommunication. Do not let these go by the wayside. Address them, and go a step further; ensure that you have systems in place to allow them to give you feedback on what you have communicated on a regular basis.

We have discussed some ideas like regular meetings and evaluations; however, I also want you to think of things like presentation evaluation sheets and suggestion boxes. These don't have to fit the traditional mode that you are used to. They could be as simple as an email poll on a single question or a pop quiz over a new topic that you introduced to keep the feedback fun and light. But the important thing is that you have those feedback points built into your system. Otherwise, you won't know if your team is truly understanding the vision you have and the ideas you are communicating until it is too late.

Growing Pains

One of the other issues that you will face as you are trying to develop into an Empowering Leader is figuring out the balance between maintaining your reputation for excellence while at the same time allowing a safe space for your team to grow while you are restructuring your team dynamics. My recommendation is that you take some time to really determine what you're trying to accomplish. For some people, you may realize that you are not ready to make the journey to becoming an Empowering Leader; this just isn't for you. That's okay. Understanding that will allow you to have the type of conversation that you need to have with your superiors so that you can remove yourself from that role.

If you are ready and you know the Leader's Way is your journey, then you need to have the conversation with your stakeholders (i.e. superiors, partners, customers, etc.) that alerts them to the fact that there is going to be a period of time where performance may not meet the expectations that you have cultivated to this point. You will entreat them to trust in you. Let them know that you are working on something that will greatly improve your team's performance. Create the space for your team to get better by measuring your superior's expectations. Very rarely will you find the stakeholder that is opposed to you taking initiative and working to improve performance and productivity.

I say all this because I want you to know that it is important for you to choose this path. That is because you need to be aware that in the short-term your reputation might suffer. You might have some work that comes out a little bit less impressive than what is expected. This is where your trust in yourself and the system must kick in. This is where you remember that you are not the type of person to ever suck at anything for long. This is where having a mentor is an invaluable resource. And this is where a quote that I love from Zig Ziglar comes in handy. He often said, "Anything worth doing is worth doing poorly until you get it." You must do the work. It is not going to come easy, but it will come.

Significant Trust Deficit

For many leaders, there is a significant trust deficit that they must overcome. This transition will only serve to exacerbate that deficit if not external influences are not handled properly. As we discussed, you have the responsibility to ensure that you create a safe space for your team to develop. This means that you must anticipate the pressures that they may receive from those outside the team during the transition.

By doing this, you help to erase the trust deficit that exists between most employees and their bosses. You begin to show them that they are what is important to you, not the esteem of your superiors/clients or peers. This is how you ensure that they are willing to protect you by working hard and doing more than they have ever done. By placing them as a priority, you create a dynamic on your team that is difficult to defeat. You create the type of team that people love to be on, one where everyone works hard to ensure the success of the team and where everyone is celebrated and where everyone's worth is valued.

This is another place where having a mentor is immeasurably valuable. Navigating the land mines of this experience is not a walk in the park. A mentor can guide you through the nuances of the conversations and diplomacy necessary to make the transition successfully.

How to deal with incompetence and incompatibility a.k.a. What if I have to let someone go?

Now, we need to deal with the 800-pound elephant in the room: What if you have team members that just won't get with the program? Or worse, what if you have team members that are just incompatible with what you are trying to build?

Well, I will tell you that these two problems need to be dealt with, and they need to be dealt with properly. However, I can also tell you that these two scenarios, like most worst-case scenarios, are unlikely to happen. While we don't want to spend a lot of time thinking about them, if we don't prepare for them, they will consume our subconscious minds until we feel safe. So let's look at these situations in order of likelihood of occurrence:

1. Incompetence: where someone can't get better
2. Incompatibility: where someone doesn't fit in with your values and isn't willing to conform

The answer to Incompetence: There are no bad students, only poor teachers.

When I was a teacher, I used to always explain to my students that I don't like giving F's. I let them know that I have set up my class so that it was nigh impossible for anyone who doesn't want to get an F to get one. I also let them know that I had set up my system such that they would never have any doubt where they were. Finally, I let them know that since I had set everything up the way I had, if they finished the period with an F, then they needed to wear that with pride because they had worked hard for it, and they deserved it.

Now, of course, I always said this tongue-in-cheek, but I was serious about the last point. If someone earned an F in my class that meant they earned it. I am happy to say that in the five years after I developed that system, no one earned an F in my class.

So how do you apply this? I always felt that if my students were near failing then so was I as their leader. I ensured that I had enough backup systems in place that if they were struggling, they could find help. What type of systems? I had after school tutoring sessions. I allowed them to take tests until they could pass them. I called parents at the midterm period of the semester for anyone who had a D or below. I sent emails and letters home. I frequently ensured that they were aware of their grades throughout the marking period. I did all of these things so that they were always aware and knew they could fix it if they wanted to. It was never going to be a surprise. And no, this did not take a whole bunch of extra time. Because I employed many of the principles in this book in my classroom, I was able to get much of this work done during the school day or my planning period.

You should do the same in your office. As we discussed before, evaluations and improvement plans should be routine. Meetings are essential. The QC checks that you do, the debriefs, the individual meetings, the reward sessions are all meant to give people an idea of where they are and, more importantly, how they can get help if they need it.

Every once in a while, however, you will have a person that doesn't want to pull their weight or just is not a fit for your team. Because you have so many objective measures to evaluate performance, the decision of what to do with them becomes easy. It is unemotional, and you can and should make it without hesitation. They need to find their way somewhere else, and your other team members should not have to carry the burden of their poor performance.

The Answer to Incompatibility: Set Them free!

While an Empowering Leader is capable of leading anyone, leadership is about leading those who want to be led. Remember, it is a helping relationship. If someone has decided that they do not want to improve and they don't want to go where you and your team are going, then you must allow them to make that choice. Even more so if the person is intentionally sabotaging your efforts, either passively or actively. For the good of the rest of the team, you must allow them to make that choice elsewhere.

And here is the key point: Do not believe that being on your team is the best place for everyone. It is not. People bring with them all types of baggage that is outside of your control. Remember: We must focus on the controllables. You get to determine who is and is not a fit. You get to determine what is and is not success. You get to determine how much your programs and systems allow for the growth of your people.

However, they get to determine whether your team is where they want to be. As Jim Collins and Jerry Poppas explain in Built to Last, the companies and teams that are built to leave a legacy are not for everyone. They are for the people that have those same values and same goals. Everyone will not want to go where you are going.

However, as the leader of one of those teams, it is just as important that you help the people who realize that this is not the team for them to make their transition well. The fact that they are not a good fit for you team does not mean they are not a good fit anywhere. They still have talents to use and greatness to manifest. They may just need to do so elsewhere. And that's okay.

Trust the System

Ultimately, your biggest challenge is going to be trusting the system. Things are going to be uncomfortable in the beginning. You are going to have to be new at something again, probably for the first time in a long time. You are going to have to channel your inner apprentice, your inner learner and delight in the experience. There is an old Chinese saying that I used to have in my classroom that said, "The Master at anything was once only a Beginner." Understand that; embrace that. It will make the journey a much more enjoyable one.

SECTION 4: LEGACY

Conclusion

> *"I really believe a champion is defined, not by their wins, but by how they recover when they fall."* -- Serena Williams
>
> *"It's not whether you get knocked down but whether you get back up."* -- Vince Lombardi

Cultivating Resiliency Is the True Key to Empowering Leadership

Much of what we discussed in the previous chapters has been centered around creating the space for you to develop your own personal resiliency and that of your team. That's because the goal is to get to the point where there are no worst-case scenarios. That is when you can be like the generals that Sun Tzu discussed in *The Art of War*. That is when you can attack and focus on winning.

You have to have faith in your people and trust that they will be able to figure it out. Leadership is about relationships. Remember that trust and faith are tremendously important to your ability to lead others. They are foundational. You must believe in your team, and more importantly, you must believe in your ability to lead them. As I have said before, you have to trust the process.

The purpose of a Leader is not to create more followers but rather to create more Leaders. As we move along the path from Executing Leader to Empowering Leader to Legacy Leader, we increase our ability to impact the world for generations. This journey is only possible if we can embrace the fact that we are going to make many mistakes along the way.

As you begin to think about how to implement this strategy where you are, I want to leave you with a story of this transition that will hopefully aid you in cultivating the resiliency you will need for this journey. But before that, I want to let you know that you are not on your own. I understand that possibly the toughest challenge of this process is to change your mindset and your paradigm. It is not easy, and it is not something that will happen overnight. I want you to know that I believe in you, and I know that you can get there. But I also want you to know that I am here to help.

If you think that you might want to work with me, go over to **www.legacyleadershipmastery.com** and let me know about your situation.

Remember that you are only a beginner at this next step of Empowering Leadership. You are learning to master a skill set that will exponentially increase your impact, your efficiency, your compassion, your empathy, and ultimately your legacy. As you continue to learn this craft, you will get better and better, and you will develop your efficacy in helping others to get the same success you have enjoyed faster and faster. This is where you will begin to transition to being a Legacy Leader, a leader who creates other Leaders.

You will move from the realm of teaching people to be awesome fisherman to becoming one of the best trainers of the trainers. People who leave your teams will go on to create leaders of their own. You will leave a legacy of teachers that will change the world.

You might have heard the saying, "Those who can't do teach." Nothing could be further from the truth. In order to truly teach and not just be a charlatan, you have to be good at doing. The reality that I hope you have come to see in this book is that those that can't teach must do. And since they can't teach, they must do more and more the better they get at doing. Trust the system, and you will become a great teacher and ultimately a Legacy Leader.

I want to leave you in this chapter with two stories that will hopefully encourage you along your path. One is the story of a friend of mine, Josh.

The Reluctant Leader

Josh owns a Real Estate Development company that specializes in custom built homes. He has run his company for about ten years now and he really started his Empowering Leadership journey about five or six years ago.

Before he began to transition to being an Empowering Leader, he was already a successful business owner. He did everything the way you are supposed to. He went to college, majoring in business and construction management. He worked on crews during the summer to learn the trade. After college, he got a job with one of the big home builders and did pretty well until that builder went under during the crash of 2008. He then decided to go out on his own and cut his teeth as an entrepreneur.

As Josh continued to build his business, he also started a family. He loved being on his job sites doing the work. And he didn't mind the extra time he had to spend because he loved what he did. But he could see that this would not be sustainable as his family grew. He began to hire people, but he loved doing the work and didn't really want to let that go. He was doing a lot of the work and the managing of the sites when he broke his wrist.

Josh spent nine months without being able to swing a hammer because of complications with his injury. During this time, he was forced to look at leading a different way. He couldn't be out there to fix everything, and he needed to do something different if his business was going to survive. And so Josh began studying how to delegate and how to empower his people to do more. He admits that this was not easy at first and is still not easy. But, when I interviewed him for this book, he made sure to point out his sincere belief that his business could not have done anywhere near the numbers that it has done over the last five years had he not been forced to change.

He is able to do more and his people have a greater passion for their work. And it is only getting better. As he gets better at setting them up to play in their strengths, he is amazed at the things they come up with that he would never have thought of or that he thought would not work until they showed him. He is coming into his stride, and he is loving where his business is going. He gets to wake up every day and do what he loves, and he gets to do it while empowering other people to be the best that they can be.

Legacy Leaders

I have alluded to the Gracies many times in this book, and this is because of the profound impact they have had not only on my life but on the world. And while I have told you about the teaching methodologies I have learned from them, the thing I want you to focus on in this section is how they exemplify what Legacy Leadership looks like in real life. In 1925, the Gracie Brothers, Grandmasters Carlos and Helio, started the Gracie Jiu Jitsu Academy in Brazil. Their focus was on teaching self-defense in a way that anyone could learn. The goal was not to create the toughest fighters in the world, although that was a byproduct of their training. The goal was to be the best teachers in the world, to empower the most students.

The qualifications to become a Gracie Jiu Jitsu instructor, then and now, were very exacting and focused on more than just one's proficiency in Jiu Jitsu. They focused on how much the teacher cared for their students, if the teacher set a good example or not, and how well the teacher could influence and instruct the least talented students. Those were the marks of a good teacher, a good leader.

Nearly 100 years later, the Gracie family Legacy includes a network of teachers that spans the globe and their impact is undeniable. Grandmaster Rorion (Helio's oldest son) created the

UFC, which is now a worldwide phenomenon. My instructors Ryron and Rener Gracie (sons of Rorion, grandsons of Grandmaster Helio) routinely hold classes at their Torrance, California Academy, the Gracie Jiu Jitsu World Headquarters, that top 100 students. There are over 120 schools around the world where students of all ages, male and female, learn to defend themselves and have more confidence in their lives and their decisions every day. They help people face whatever challenges life can throw at them because they create a safe space for getting knocked down and learning how to get back up.

This Legacy includes a Gracie Certified Training Center in Jacksonville, NC that is very special to me. It represents part of my own personal Leadership Legacy. I started this school a little over two years ago at the time I am writing this, and it is still going strong even though I have not been at the helm for nearly a year. My students have become the teachers, and they are now the ones helping others to develop their gifts and cultivate their resiliency.

This is the type of Legacy you can have. This is the type of impact you can have if you focus on empowering those that you teach, creating a safe space for them to fail, and cultivating their ability to bounce back from anything.

***

I want to thank you for sticking with me this far. Hopefully, over the time you have been reading this book, you have been able to see two things: 1) Leadership is about much more than simply accomplishing objectives, and 2) you have what it takes to be a great and Empowering Leader.

I truly believe that Legacy Leadership is our greatest calling. To develop our talents and our compassion to the point where we are able to aid others in their development and then pass that on is the pinnacle of achievement. It is not enough to accomplish great things. It is not enough to lead others to accomplish great things. Our job as Legacy Leaders is to prepare the way for those that come after us and then to teach them to do the same. Becoming an Empowering Leader is the next step along that path.

As you continue your journey, always strive to be the type of leader that creates other leaders. Ultimately, your Leadership Legacy is not the accomplishments that you leave behind, it is the leaders you leave behind. Your impact on the world is defined by how many people you've helped to impact the lives of others.

Often times, this seems like a daunting task. And many times we may not think we are up to it or qualified for it. If you struggle with Imposter Syndrome and perfectionism like I did, you may not feel worthy of it. But this is your calling. You have been blessed to be good at what you do. You have put your work ethic and your character to the test, and you have risen to the ranks of leadership. Now is your time to realize the platform that you have to make a tremendous impact on the world in the present and on future generations.

The work that you do as a leader has a greater impact than you know. It will impact the way that the people you lead treat other people in their lives. It will affect how people parent, how they engage in relationships, how they trust, how they apply themselves, and ultimately how they lead. And that is why it is imperative that those of us who are fortunate enough to lead other people remember those words that Marianne Williamson spoke in her book *A Course in Miracles*.

"Our deepest fear is not that we are inadequate. Our deepest fear is that we are powerful beyond measure. It is our light, not our darkness, that most frightens us. We ask ourselves, "Who am I to be brilliant, gorgeous, talented, and fabulous? Actually, who are you not to be? You are a child of God. Your playing small does not serve the world. There is nothing enlightened about shrinking so that other people will not feel insecure around you. We are all meant to shine, as children do. We were born to make manifest the glory of God that is within us. It is not just in some of us; it is in everyone and as we let our own light shine, we unconsciously give others permission to do the same. As we are liberated from our own fear, our presence automatically liberates others."

I call on you as a leader to internalize the meaning of those words for you and your team. You must realize the greatness that lies within you and the purpose for that greatness. It is not for your glory; it is to impact the world. By you shining, by you living in your purpose, by you being the best Leader you can be, you give permission to all those that you lead to grow on that path. By showing them that you care for and trust them, by showing them that you believe in their abilities and that you have faith in them, you liberate them from the fear of failure and serve as a beacon of light calling them into their greatness.

One of the things that I realize as I look back upon my journey is that all along the way, I have had amazing mentors and leaders who showed me how. For so much of my life I have had leaders who I knew believed in me and allowed me the room to make mistakes and grow. Because of them, I am the man I am today. This is what I hope those that I lead can say about me, and this is my reason for writing this book. So that one day, those that you lead can say that about you.

***

So, there you have it. The EMPOWER Method is there for you to use as you will. You now have all you need to continue to develop your Leader's Heart, Mind, and Toolkit, and become the type of Empowering Leader that I know that you can be. I want to thank you for the time you have spent reading this book and for the energy you have spent working towards being a better leader. The world is a better place because of your dedication to your people. I want you to know that I appreciate you.

If you are the type of learner that does well studying from a book but you know you would get so much more from working with a mentor, then I want you to reach out to me and my team. We will get on the phone and work to see in what way we can best serve you on your Leadership journey. You can also go to https://www.facebook.com/groups/LegacyLeaders2018/, join my #LegacyLeaders group and get access to the seven-part video series, The EMPOWER Method. Lastly, check out my event calendar and the next time I am in your area, come out and see me. I want to hear your story.

I want you to know that you don't have to be in a rush to get there, but you do have get started. As Les Brown says, "You don't have be great to get started, but you do have to get started to be great!" Go find a mentor and get started as soon as possible, for it will take time to master this next stage of the journey. Continue to love and care for your people. Continue to set them up for success. Continue to engage their inner problem solver. If you do these things, then you will be well on your way to being a Legacy Leader. You have embarked on becoming the type of Leader that, when your task is accomplished, when your work is finished, your people will say, "We Did It Ourselves!"

Acronym Glossary

EMPOWER

EXAMINE AND EVALUATE YOUR EXPECTATIONS

MEASURE EXPECTATIONS

PROPER DELEGATION

OPTIMIZE YOUR ENVIRONMENT FOR GROWTH

WATCH AND LEARN

ENGAGE THEIR INNER PROBLEM SOLVER

REWARD WHAT YOU WANT TO CONTINE

SWOT

STRENGTHS

WEAKNESSES

OPPORTUNITIES

THREATS

BAMCIS

BEGIN PLANNING

ARRANGE RECONNAISANCE

MAKE RECONNAISANCE

COMPLETE PLANNING

IMPLEMENT PLAN

SUPERVISE

SMART

SPECIFIC

MEASURABLE

ATTAINABLE

RELEVANT

TIME-BOUND

5 PRINCIPLES OF DELEGATION

CLARITY

ASPIRATION

INSPIRATION

TRUST

OWNERSHIP

Further Reading

Expect to Win by Carla Harris

Helping by Edgar Schein

Rich Dad, Poor Dad by Robert Kiyosaki

How to Win Friends and Influence People by Dale Carnegie

Built to Last by Jim Collins and Jerry Poppas

Start with Why by Simon Sinek

On Leadership by John Wooden

Acknowledgments

There are so many people that I need to thank for making this happen. I want to begin with my wife and my kids. Thank you for understanding how important this work was to me and making all the accommodations to let me write. I know that not knocking on the door and keeping it quiet in the living room were not easy, but it is tremendously appreciated. We did it!

Next, to my mentor, Dr. Angela Lauria, and all my fellow authors at The Author Incubator, thank you for your guidance, your support, your love. Special thanks to Dr. Angela for your creating a safe space for so many of us who have messages that we need to bring forth. It is truly a transformational process, and I am so thankful for the help I received becoming the author who wrote this book. I also want to thank the team over at the Author Incubator for their work on this project. Cheyenne, Ora, Todd, and the crew. You all are tremendously appreciated. You are amazing to work with.

To all of those who believed in this project and funded it, I also say thank you. Joe, Jamal, Reggie, Karen, Doug, and Jim. You all made this possible. You were the first believers and the first to be willing to walk down this path with me. I want to thank you so much for your help, your support, and your investment.

To all of my supporters, friends, and well-wishers who have been there to give me guidance and love. Thank you so much. To my book launch team: Thank you for your support and your feedback.

To all of my friends and mentors, Josh M., Jay H., Ken B., Ken H., Josh H., Ron, David, Josh the Builder, and H. Walker. Thank you for your guidance and your wisdom. It was always helpful to be able to bounce ideas off of you and to know that you had my best interest at heart when I came to you with questions.

To all of the leaders I have had in my life. Most of you have been amazing, and I thank you for showing me the way to lead from a place of love and caring for your people. So many of the things that I learned under your care make up the lessons in this book. This is your #LeadershipLegacy

And to those of my leaders who were not so great at it, I thank you as well. I know that for each of you, you had your own struggles, and I can say that I truly believe you were doing your best. Thank you for allowing me to learn from your experience; you have made me a better leader. Perhaps this book can help you to achieve your desires and to improve your Leadership Legacy.

To my parents, thank you for you the love you have given me all my life. Thank you for always inspiring me to be the best I could be and supporting me whenever I decided to do something. I always knew that you believed in me, most times way more than I believed in myself. Without your example and your love, I would not be the man I am today.

And finally, a special thanks again to my wife, Wendy. You have been the person in this world, aside from my parents, who has had unwavering faith in me. You have pulled me through times where it was so hard to believe. You have shown me the power of vulnerability and faith and helped me to strengthen my faith in the goodness of people. Thank you for being such a tremendous example of loyalty and faith. I love you, and I thank you for being my first follower, my biggest fan, and my most ardent cheerleader. We did it, baby!

About the Author

Robert Heath, Sr. is an engaging communicator and leading expert in Empowering Leadership. His work is centered on helping people find their passion, empowering them to achieve their dreams, and giving them the tools to empower others to do the same.

Robert received his JD, *cum laude,* from the University of Illinois College of Law. He also holds an MA in Teaching from Christian Brother's University, as well as dual BA degrees in Economics and Speech Communications from the University of Illinois at Urbana-Champaign. He served for 8 years as a United States Marine Corps Officer, receiving the Navy and Marine Corps Commendation Medal for his leadership as a Commander of one of the largest companies in the Marine Corps.

Over the past 20 years, he has served in many leadership roles across various industries. During this time, he has helped thousands of people discover the leader within. From his time as a Spanish teacher and a basketball coach, to his record-setting efforts as an attorney, to his award-winning work as a Company Commander, Robert has worked to embody the proverb Aristotle spoke so long ago, that "excellence is a habit rather than the result of a single action."

Robert believes that his career, his accomplishments, and his success in life are the proof that no matter who you are, or where you come from, everyone is capable of developing that same habit of excellence. His leadership training is grounded in this idea and in his belief that with the proper guidance, everyone has the capacity to develop these habits in themselves, and in others.

He is the Founder of the Legacy Empowerment Academy and the CEO of Legacy Leadership Consulting. Combining the leadership principles he learned as an Officer and Company Commander in the Marine Corps with the personnel development strategies he has mastered over 20 years of leading, teaching, and coaching, Robert works with leaders who desire to increase initiative and follow-through, reduce stress, and get the very best out of their team on every project, regardless of who they may lead.

Robert's most important accomplishment is being a loving husband and father. He lives with his family in Grand Rapids, MI.

For more about Robert visit www.legacyleadershipmastery.com; email him at robert@legacyleadershipmastery.com; or find him on Facebook at www.facebook.com/groups/LegacyLeaders2018/.

Thank You

Thank you for allowing me to guide you along on your leadership journey. I truly appreciate the trust that you placed in my efforts, and I hope that this book has given you some things to think about as well as some tips and strategies to use with your teams. I want you to know that I understand that there was a lot of information in this book and that is why I created my companion program, The Leader's Way™. If you would like to work with me and have me help you go through the strategies that I discuss in the book with you and your team, then feel free to reach out and schedule a strategy session with me. You can simply go to www.legacyleadershipmastery.com

Thanks again and may your Leadership Journey be enlightening and fulfilling!

Made in the USA
Columbia, SC
04 January 2020